CAMBRIDGE

Foundation

MATHEMATICS
GCSE for Edexcel
Problem-solving Book

Tabitha Steel, Coral Thomas, Mark Dawes and Steven Watson

CAMBRIDGE
UNIVERSITY PRESS

University Printing House, Cambridge CB2 8BS, United Kingdom

Cambridge University Press is part of the University of Cambridge.

It furthers the University's mission by disseminating knowledge in the pursuit of education, learning and research at the highest international levels of excellence.

www.cambridge.org
Information on this title:
www.cambridge.org/ukschools/9781107450066 (Paperback)

First published 2015

Printed in the United Kingdom by Latimer Trend

A catalogue record for this publication is available from the British Library

ISBN 978-1-107-45006-6 Paperback

Additional resources for this publication at www.cambridge.org/ukschools

Cover image © 2013 Fabian Oefner www.fabianoefner.com

Contents

Introduction

What is a mathematical problem?

In everyday speech you might talk about a 'problem' as being something that is negative and often annoying. It might also be referred to as a difficulty, or as something that needs to be fixed.

Mathematical problems might be difficult, they might even be annoying, but they are certainly not negative! Some people see mathematical problems as any sort of mathematical question and some people use 'problem' in this way. 2 + 3 is quite a simple question. 117 × 495 is more difficult but it is still just a question (even though some people will not know how to work it out).

The definition of a mathematical problem used in this book is: something you don't know how to solve immediately.

117 × 495 could be worked out by writing down the number 117, adding on 117, and adding on another 117 again and again until you have written it 495 times. Even if you don't have a quicker way of working this out (and it would be a good idea to have a quicker way!) then this is not actually mathematical problem-solving.

You often need to think 'around' a problem before you can get started.

A mathematical problem, then, is likely to be challenging, and it might well be the case that you can't 'see' the answer quickly. There are lots of things that might help you though, and this book will show you some of those ideas.

Different types of mathematics

To be able to do maths you need to know and understand mathematical ideas. These are important, and Cambridge University Press's *GCSE Mathematics for Edexcel Foundation Student Book* covers this sort of material. You also need to be able to solve problems, and this can be more difficult.

Problem-solving 'muscle memory'

When you learn to do something new you usually have to think very hard about what you are doing. For example, when someone first learns to drive a car they have to concentrate hard and decide which foot to press down, which way to move the gear stick, which mirror to look in, and so on. Experienced motorists still need to concentrate on the road, but they don't need to think about the mechanics of every single action they take. This is known as 'muscle memory'. Muscle memory comes up lots in sports, so a footballer might have to train hard to learn how to do a rainbow flick, but will then be able to do it without thinking about it.

When you solve an equation the answer itself is often not very exciting ("$x = 3$... big deal!"). The important thing when solving lots of equations is not finding out whether x happens to be 3 or 4 this time around, but that you are putting equation-solving in your muscle memory. Some of the problems you solve in this book **will** be interesting in their own right. We hope you will enjoy the challenge of doing them and will enjoy the answers too. Beyond this, though, you should not just work out the answers and be satisfied with that. After each problem, try to reflect on how you solved it. It is important to think about this, because this is the point at which you will learn new skills and this is how the muscle memory will start to develop.

Impossible to obvious

At first, a mathematical problem may appear to be impossible. When you know the answer or when you know how to do it, the problem can then seem obvious and not worth thinking about.

Hopefully you will avoid both of these extremes. None of the problems you will be asked to solve in this book are 'impossible' – do see them as a challenge. Even if a problem is obvious to you it is still likely to involve important ideas that you might be able to apply to other, more challenging problems in the future.

Year 3000 by *Busted* has the chorus lyric:

"I've been to the year 3000. ...

And your great, great, great granddaughter

Is pretty fine."

You might be concerned about the number of 'great's in the lyric.

How do we know we need more 'great's? How many 'great's should there be?

Start working on this problem by yourself. Once you've finished, talk to other people about what you have done.

How to use this book

Each chapter in this book covers a problem-solving strategy – a way of approaching a problem. The chapter starts by describing the strategy and how to apply it to a problem. This is followed by questions which you can solve by applying that strategy.

Each question covers one or more strands of maths, which is shown by the colour wheel beside the question number.

The exploded pieces(s) of the colour wheel tells you what strand(s) of maths each question covers:

Number

Algebra

Ratio, proportion and rates of change

Geometry and measures

Probability

Statistics

The questions have been written to give you regular practice at problem solving so that you can build your skills, confidence and mathematical experience not only for your GCSE exams but also for life outside the classroom.

The star rating suggests the amount of problem-solving experience needed to tackle each question.

⭐️ 1 star questions are 'entry-level', they are good questions to start with.

⭐️⭐️ 2 star questions are ideal to move on to when you have confidently and successfully completed some of the entry-level questions.

⭐️⭐️⭐️ 3 star questions are for when you need more of a challenge.

In other words, the more stars, the more difficult the question is.

This means that you might need a calculator to work through the problem.

This means that you should work through a question without a calculator. If this symbol is not present, you can use a calculator if you want.

Tip

Tip boxes provide hints to help you work through questions.

Worked solutions to all the questions are provided at the back of the book. Blue boxes next to the solutions guide you through the working.

There is an old saying: 'A picture is worth a thousand words.'

So, if a diagram is not provided then draw one. It might be helpful, and could give you some ideas about how to solve the problem.

Draw a decent diagram. A sketch is probably fine, but it needs to look like the situation it describes. If there is a triangle in the problem, then your shape should be a triangle. If there is supposed to be a straight line then your line should be straight. The actual sizes of sides and angles are probably not important. Try to make your diagrams large and clear.

Annotate your diagram. If there is information provided in the question (such as the lengths of sides, or the sizes of angles) then write these on your diagram. This will often help when you are solving a problem.

Add new information that you work out. When you work out something new, add this to the diagram too.

So, in summary:
- draw a decent diagram
- annotate it
- add new information that you work out.

Here is a problem:

A farmer has 22 fence panels and wants to use them to make a rectangular enclosure for his sheep. How many different enclosures can he make?

A picture of a field with sheep and lambs in it will not be helpful here.

Instead, a diagram of a rectangle would be more useful.

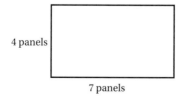

4 panels

7 panels

Now you can finish off this question.

Two of the sides add up to 11 (because the perimeter is 22 panels).

The dimensions that are possible are:

1 by 10	3 by 8	5 by 6
2 by 9	4 by 7	So he can make 5 different enclosures.

It is fairly obvious what to do when a diagram has been provided as part of a question, but a diagram can sometimes be useful in other situations. Here is another example where drawing diagrams could help you.

At a fast food restaurant there is a 'meal deal' that involves first choosing one of the following: cheeseburger, chicken burger, veggie burger or salad, and then ordering a side dish from the following list: fries, baked potato or coleslaw.

How many different meals could you have?

You could work systematically and create a list, but a diagram would also help.

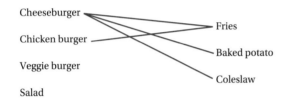

The diagram above shows all the options and the lines show some of the possible combinations.

There are three lines coming from cheeseburger. How many lines will come from chicken burger when the diagram is finished? Will this help you answer the question?

Alternatively, you could create a table like the one below to help you. What does each cell in this table represent? How does this table tell you, at a glance, how many meal possibilities there are?

	Fries	Baked potato	Coleslaw
Cheeseburger			
Chicken burger			
Veggie burger			
Salad			

The following problems may be solved using more than one method; however, the worked solutions provided at the back of this book are based on the method introduced above.

A rectangle has length $(2x + 3)$ cm and width $(x - 1)$ cm.

The perimeter of the rectangle is 70 cm.

a Write an expression for the perimeter of the rectangle.

b How long is the longest side?

c Work out the area of the rectangle.

Ajit is making a lampshade, based on the design shown. The lampshade consists of three cylinders covered in fabric.

How much fabric will Ajit need to make this lampshade?

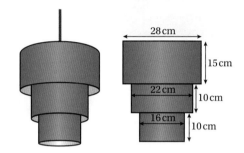

Tip

You need to calculate the surface area of each cylinder in the lampshade. Remember that each cylinder is covered with a rectangle of fabric.

How much fabric is required to construct a tent, like the one shown below? The top vertex is above the middle of the square base.

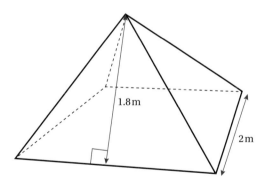

Tip

What shapes do you need? Draw them and label them.

Margaret's garden contains lavender bushes and geraniums. There is a row of six lavender bushes, then a row of ten geraniums, then six lavenders, then ten geraniums, etc.

The rows alternate and finish with a row of lavender.

There are 70 geranium plants.

How many lavender plants are there?

Peter the factory manager planned to install a new hot drinks machine for the factory workers. He decided to fill it with tea as he thought tea was the most popular hot drink among the workers.

The workers did a survey to check what their preferred hot drinks were. Each person surveyed could choose one drink from hot chocolate, tea and coffee.

8 women wanted hot chocolate. 16 workers wanted tea, of which 7 were men. 10 men and 12 women chose coffee. There were 25 men in total.

Was Peter correct?

Tip

What type of diagram would be useful here?

Here are the mock exam results (out of 100) in GCSE Mathematics and GCSE Statistics for a group of students (represented by letters A–L) .

	A	B	C	D	E	F	G	H	I	J	K	L
Mathematics	68	62	50	54	86	65	74	60	54	39	48	
Statistics	73	68	54	62	87	71	32	65	59	57	53	70

Tip

What type of diagram could you draw to help you see the link between the Maths and Statistics results?

Student L sat the GCSE Statistics examination and achieved a score of 70 but was ill during the GCSE Mathematics examination and could not complete the paper.

a Predict the Mathematics result for Student L.

b How good is your prediction likely to be?

c What is the statistical term for student G?

Granny Bessie is making a patchwork quilt with scraps of fabric.

Tip

The diagram in the question is very detailed. Could a simpler diagram help?

Each patch is $(2x - 3)$ cm long and $(x + 3)$ cm wide.

a There are 25 patches in each row. Write a possible expression for the width of the quilt.

b There are 32 patches in each column. Write a possible expression for the length of the quilt.

The width of each patch is 8 cm.

c Calculate the dimensions of the quilt. Give your answer in metres.

In a cement factory, the cement bags are placed on pallets made of planks of wood and bricks as shown in the diagram below.

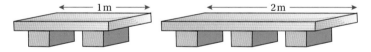

The number of bricks needed to make the pallet is calculated as 'one more than the length of the plank in metres'.

a What length of pallet uses five bricks?

b If a pallet is 3 m long, how many bricks does it use?

The factory needs pallets with a total length of 15 m for its next batch of cement. It has planks of wood that are 4 m long and 3 m long.

c What combinations of planks can they have?

d How many bricks would they need for each combination?

Sophie has a sheet of rainbow paper and she wants to use it to cover a box. The box is in the shape of a cuboid without a lid.

Its dimensions are 20 cm by 10 cm and it has a height of 8 cm.

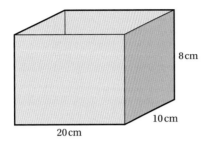

8 cm

10 cm

20 cm

a What is the surface area of the five exterior faces of the box?

The walls of the box are 5 mm thick. Sophie would like to cover the inside of the box as well, but not the inside of the base.

Her sheet of paper measures 45 cm by 55 cm.

b Is the sheet of paper big enough for Sophie to cover the outside and inside walls of her box?

In cycling races, hill climbs are rated according to a category system. A category 5 climb is the easiest; it has an average slope of 3 : 100 (for every 100 m horizontal distance you climb 3 m vertically).

a What is the angle of the slope in a category 5 climb?

The hardest category of climb has an average slope of 1 : 10.

b How much steeper is this climb compared with the category 5 climb in degrees?

Ann-Marie wants to plant a cherry tree in her garden.

She knows that when it is fully grown it will have a diameter of 3 m.

Ann-Marie wants all of the fruit to fall on her lawn.

Here is a sketch, not to scale, of Ann-Marie's garden.

Tip

This diagram isn't drawn to scale, but your diagram should be.

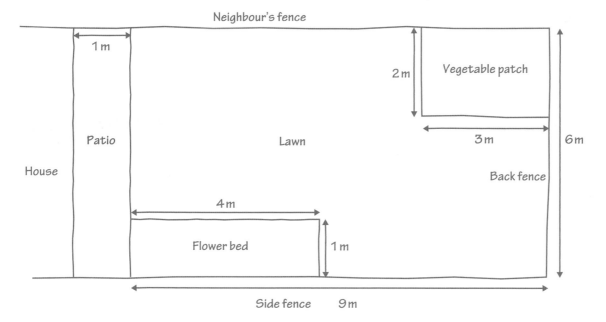

Where could the tree be planted?

The diagram represents two remote towns labelled A and B.

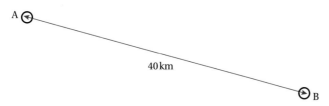

The mountain rescue helicopters from both towns will always be dispatched to rescue any casualty within a radius of 25 km of town A or town B. The fire brigade from town B will travel to any accident scene closer to town B than town A.

Shade the region that the helicopters and town B's fire brigade will both cover.

The vertices of a quadrilateral are A, B, C and D.

A has coordinates $(2, 1)$.

$$\overrightarrow{AB} = \begin{pmatrix} 2 \\ 3 \end{pmatrix}, \overrightarrow{BC} = \begin{pmatrix} 4 \\ 0 \end{pmatrix}, \overrightarrow{AD} = \begin{pmatrix} 4 \\ 0 \end{pmatrix}$$

a Write a column vector for $\overrightarrow{CD}$.

b Compare $\overrightarrow{CD}$ with $\overrightarrow{AB}$. What do you notice? Can you explain?

c What type of quadrilateral is $ABCD$?

Tip

Draw the shape on squared paper.

Geoff and Ravinder are very competitive and often play badminton and squash matches. The probability of Geoff winning at badminton is 0.85 and the probability of Geoff winning at squash is 0.35.

a What is the probability that the next time they play both badminton and squash, Geoff wins both matches?

b What is the probability that Geoff loses at badminton but wins at squash?

c What is the probability that Geoff and Ravinder win one match each?

Tip

Try different values, even scores or 50–50.

The probability Leela catches the 6.30 am train to Brighton is 0.7. If she misses the train she will be late for work.

The probability the train will be late is 0.15. If the train is late she will be late for work.

What is the probability Leela will be on time for work on a particular day?

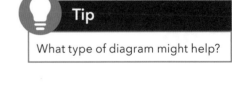

Tip

What type of diagram might help?

A projector is placed 1 m from a screen. When the projector is turned on, the image produced on the screen is only 20 cm high.

How far back should the projector be moved in order to produce an image that fills the screen, which is approximately 1.5 m high? (Assume that no other adjustments are made to the projector.)

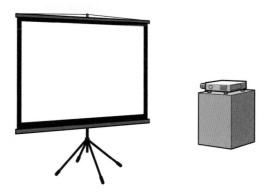

a Harriet has a challenge for her classmate Janet: Can she draw the following triangle?

- It has a right angle.

- It has one angle of 40°.

- It has one side that is 5 cm long.

  i Accurately draw a triangle that satisfies Harriet's conditions.

  ii Demonstrate that there is more than one triangle that fulfils her conditions.

  iii How could Harriet alter her challenge so that only one triangle is possible?

b Janet then comes up with a challenge for Harriet.

- Her triangle has one side that is 4 cm long.

- Another side is 7 cm.

- The angle in between these two sides is 55°.

  i How many triangles satisfy Janet's conditions? Explain why.

  ii Measure the length of the third side.

Tip

To construct an accurate triangle you may need to use a ruler, protractor and a pair of compasses.

Tip

Before you start your accurate drawing, make some sketches to show the positions of the sides and angles you are given.

Two cafes record what types of drinks they sell during a morning.

a Write a list of all types of statistical graphs or charts you know how to draw.

b Explain which graphs / charts from your list are appropriate or inappropriate.

c Draw the graph or chart you think is most appropriate and explain what it tells you.

	Frequency	
Type of drink	Shop A	Shop B
Tea	28	15
Americano	22	8
Espresso	9	6
Latte	6	35
Cappuccino	7	26

Jane left home at 09.30 and walked at a speed of 5 km/h through the park until she reached the swings, which are 1250 m from her house.

In the park she saw June playing on the swings so she stopped to play on the swings with her for 30 minutes.

After this, Jane continued the 1500 m to Julie's house. She arrived there at 11.30.

Jane stayed at Julie's house until 15.00. She then walked directly home, arriving at 16.40.

a Complete the travel graph for Jane's journey to and from Julie's house.

b At what speed did Jane walk for the second stage of her journey to Julie's house?

c What was Jane's speed on her return journey in the afternoon?

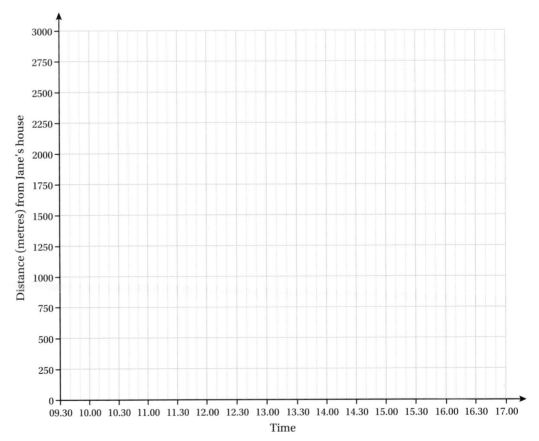

Marianne needs to make a long-distance journey. She is looking for the cheapest possible car hire. Whacky Wheels has a standard charge of £35, then 15p for every km driven. Wheelies Rentals has a charge of 23p per km travelled.

a Complete the charges graph for both car hire companies.

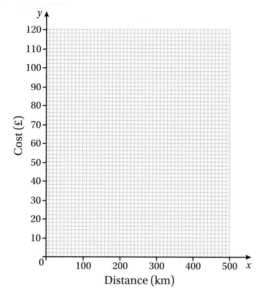

Tip

In this question you can use the axes that are given to help you draw the diagram.

b Marianne thinks the return journey is 300 km. Which company would be cheaper to use?

c Unfortunately Marianne made a mistake in her route plan and the return journey is 500 km. How much money would Marianne have saved by using the other hire company?

The probability of it raining on Tuesday is 0.15. If it rains on Tuesday, the probability of it raining on Wednesday is 0.25. If it does not rain on Tuesday, the probability of it raining on Wednesday is 0.45.

a Draw a tree diagram to show the possible outcomes.

b What is the probability it rains on both Tuesday and Wednesday?

c What is the probability it rains on only one of the days?

22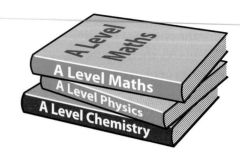

The owner of a new bookshop wanted to find out which A Level textbooks to stock so he asked 200 students if they were studying Chemistry, Physics or Maths.

43 of the students surveyed did not study any of these three subjects.

92 were studying Chemistry.

23 students were studying both Chemistry and Maths, but not Physics.

19 students were studying both Physics and Maths, but not Chemistry.

29 students were only studying Physics, and there were a total of 74 students who studied Physics.

53 of the students studied two of the three subjects.

a Display the information provided in a Venn diagram.

b If one person was chosen at random, what is the probability that they only studied Maths?

c If one person was chosen at random, what is the probability that they studied at least two of the subjects?

23

Caroline and Janet do some lane swimming every morning. They swim a total of 45 lengths each. They always start and finish together. Caroline and Janet swim at different speeds for different swimming strokes but always take 30 minutes to finish their 45 lengths.

Caroline always swims 45 lengths of breaststroke, completing each one at the same speed.

Janet always does 20 lengths of front crawl in the first 10 minutes, then the remaining 25 lengths in the rest of the time.

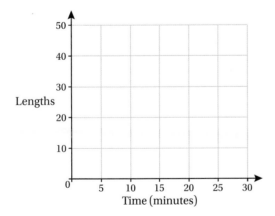

a Complete a graph for each swimmer using the axes provided.

b Is there a time when Caroline has swum more lengths than Janet?

c How long does it take Caroline to swim 30 lengths?

d What is Caroline's speed, in lengths per minute?

You are 'armed' with the three transformations listed below.

A Reflect in the line $y = x$.

B Translate by vector $\begin{pmatrix} 1 \\ 0 \end{pmatrix}$.

C Enlarge by scale factor $\frac{1}{2}$ about the point (2, 3).

a Carry out all three transformations, in order, to a starting shape of your choice.

b How does the resulting image change if the transformations are applied in reverse order C → B → A?

Tip

You will find this question easier if you actually try it out.

Think about how you can make the question simpler by choosing particular shapes and certain side lengths that make the enlargement easier.

With some problems, focusing on the answer doesn't help. Instead it is sometimes easier to work out what you **can** do rather than what you **want** to do. Sometimes, you will find you have got the answer almost by accident! Here is an example to demonstrate.

In this diagram a square and an isosceles triangle sit on a straight line. Work out the size of angle A.

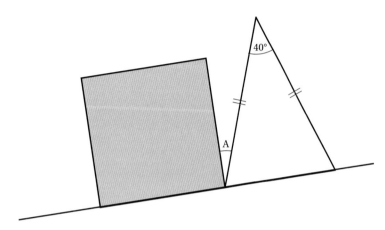

At the moment you can't work out angle A. But there are some things you **do** know.

There is a square in the diagram, so you can put in some angles.

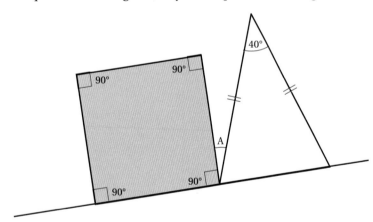

Some of these might not be helpful, but as there are only a few angles on the diagram, you are already narrowing down the problem.

Another piece of information you have got is that the triangle is isosceles. That means you can work out the other angles in the triangle. One angle is given as 40° and you know that all the angles in the triangle add up to 180°. This means the other two add up to 140° and because they are both equal they must each be 70°.

Now mark those angles on the diagram.

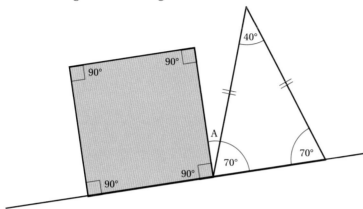

Now you can see what to do!

In the middle of the diagram there are three angles on a straight line. You know that these add up to 180° and you know what two of them are, so you can work out what angle A is.

90° + 70° = 160°   180° – 160° = 20°   So angle A = 20°

Tip

Remember
Angles on a straight line add up to 180°.

Now go back to the question.

In this diagram a square and an isosceles triangle sit on a straight line. Work out the size of angle A.

Check whether you missed out any important information. In this case, you will see that you have used all of the information provided in the question.

In this diagram a square (*you used the fact that angles in a square are 90°*) **and an isosceles triangle** (*you used the facts that base angles in an isosceles triangle are equal and that angles in a triangle add up to 180°*) **sit on a straight line** (*you used the fact that angles on a straight line add up to 180°*). **Work out the size of angle A.** (*You've done that*).

The key points are: draw a good diagram, work out the things you can, and then write this new information on the diagram.

The following problems may be solved using more than one method; however, the worked solutions provided at the back of this book are based on the method introduced above.

1

Without using a calculator, decide if the statement below is true or false.

$10\sqrt{64} < 80$

Explain your answer.

2

Andy decides to make a border for his garden using railway sleepers. He knows the length he needs is 20 m. When he gets to the garden centre he discovers each sleeper is $8\frac{1}{2}$ feet long and costs £22.

He knows that 1 foot is about 30 cm.

How much will it cost him to buy enough sleepers?

3

Karol is completely redecorating his living room. He needs to buy skirting board to put at the bottom of every wall. Karol's living room is rectangular with two doorways, each 85 cm wide.

Skirting board costs £4.31 per m.

How much will it cost Karol to buy enough skirting board?

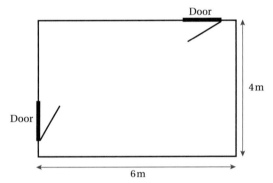

4

Mrs Jones and Miss Smith are writing topic tests for GCSE Mathematics.

Each topic test must have 32 questions split in the ratio of 3 : 5 for non-calculator to calculator questions.

a How many non-calculator questions will each topic test contain?

Mrs Jones is writing the calculator questions for 15 topic tests.

b How many questions in total must she write?

Miss Smith is writing all of the non-calculator questions and some of the calculator questions for these 15 topic tests, so that she and Mrs Jones are each writing the same number of questions.

c How many calculator questions will Miss Smith write?

d What fraction of the total questions written by Miss Smith will be calculator questions?

Jenny makes a kite. She starts from a square piece of paper, like this.

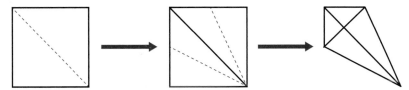

Tip

What do you know about the sides of the quadrilateral?

She then makes more kites and puts them together around a point. The start of this pattern is shown in the diagram.

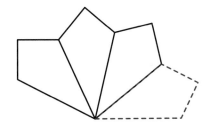

How many kites does she need altogether so that they fit together without any gaps?

The mean of 5 numbers is 12.

The numbers are in the ratio of $1:1:3:4:6$.

Find the largest number.

A space probe took approximately ten years to reach Comet 67P, which is roughly 300 million miles from Earth.

One of the fastest speeds recorded in a car was 290 miles per hour.

How many times faster was the space probe travelling?

Lola draws some shapes on square dotted paper.

Which shape is the odd one out?

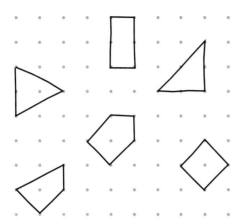

Jo creates a quadrilateral by folding a rectangular piece of paper as shown in the diagram below.

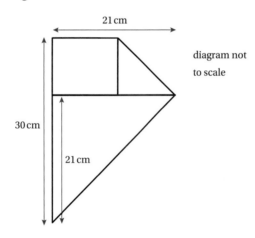

21 cm

diagram not
to scale

30 cm

21 cm

a What is the area of the quadrilateral?

b What fraction of the original rectangle does the quadrilateral represent?

a Find a formula in terms of x for the area of the shape shown below.

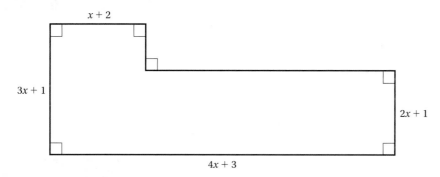

The actual length of the side labelled $3x + 1$ cm is 16 m.

b Solve the equation $3x + 1 = 16$.

c What is the area of the shape? Give your answer in square metres.

The shape is the plan of a field. Farmer Smith wants to put a fence around the field.

He plans to put three lengths of wire between wooden posts around the field, as shown in the diagram.

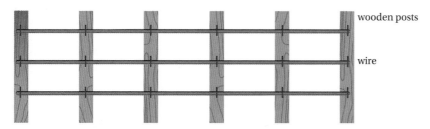

Farmer Smith will be fixing the wooden posts 1 m apart.

d How many wooden posts will Farmer Smith need, in total?

e What length of wire will Farmer Smith require for three lengths, as shown in the diagram?

Posts cost £18.50 each and wire is sold at £2.30 per m.

f How much is it going to cost Farmer Smith to fence the field?

11 ✪ ✪ ☆

The height of the water in a cylindrical tube was 12 cm. When two identical steel cubes were dropped into the tube the water level rose.

The diameter of the cylindrical tube is 8 cm.

The cubes have a side length of 4 cm.

Calculate the increase in the height of the water.

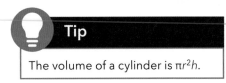
Tip

The volume of a cylinder is $\pi r^2 h$.

  12 ✪ ✪ ☆

a The image below shows the net of a triangular prism. Calculate the volume of the prism when it is constructed.

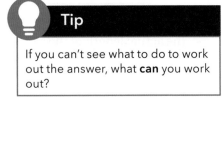
Tip

If you can't see what to do to work out the answer, what **can** you work out?

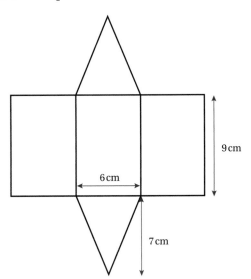

9 cm

6 cm

7 cm

b The image on the right shows the net of a different prism. When constructed, the volume of this prism is the same as the volume of the triangular prism in part **a**. Calculate the length of this prism.

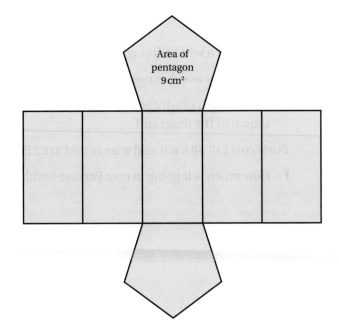

Area of pentagon 9 cm²

Jeff takes a full 500 ml bottle of water and pours himself a drink into the glass shown on the right. He fills the glass to 2 cm below the top.

How much water is left in the bottle?

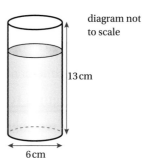

diagram not to scale

13 cm

6 cm

The teacher has a dice but doesn't know whether it is biased.
20 students each throw the dice ten times. The number of times each student rolls a six is shown below.

Is the dice biased? Explain your ideas.

Student	Number of sixes in 10 rolls
A	7
B	4
C	3
D	6
E	4
F	3
G	4
H	5
I	5
J	3
K	4
L	5
M	6
N	4
O	5
P	7
Q	0
R	3
S	3
T	2

Rectangle **A** is 2 cm long and 3 cm high.

Rectangle **B** has an area of 12 cm².

Rectangle **C** has a perimeter of 20 cm.

Rectangle **D** has a length of 4 cm and an area of 24 cm².

Explain which pair of rectangles must be mathematically similar. All four rectangles' sides and lengths are integer measurements.

 Daniel is celebrating his birthday by taking six friends paintballing. He knows it costs £4.20 per person to hire the equipment and that they will also want snacks and drinks.

Daniel's grandmother has given him £20 towards the cost of the trip and his friends will pay for the rest between them.

a Write an inequality to model this situation.

b What is the minimum amount of money that each of Daniel's friends must bring to cover the cost of the paintballing?

Tip
How much will the equipment cost to hire altogether?
How much money does Daniel have?

 $\frac{4}{5}$ of the rectangle to the right is shaded.

a How many extra unit squares must be shaded in order to increase this fraction to $\frac{5}{6}$?

The $\frac{4}{5}$-shaded rectangle is put next to a congruent rectangle that is $\frac{2}{3}$ shaded.

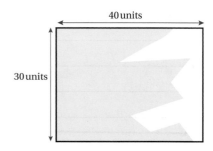

40 units

30 units

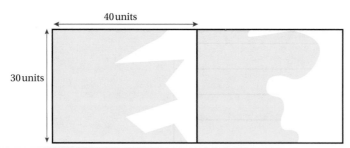

40 units

30 units

b What fraction of the resulting large rectangle is shaded?

c How many unit squares need to be shaded to increase the fraction so that exactly $\frac{3}{4}$ of the large rectangle is shaded?

Tip
Work out the area of the rectangle and then work out the shaded area. How does this help?

Javed's bike has a puncture. He knows the circumference of his tyre is approximately 220 cm. Replacement inner tubes are sized by diameter.

a What is the diameter of Javed's tyre?

A special device fixed to Javed's wheel measures the number of times the wheel turns and calculates the distance travelled.

b How far has Javed cycled when the device has measured 50 revolutions? Give your answer in metres.

c How many revolutions would the device record if Javed cycles the route shown in the diagram on the right? Give your answer to the nearest whole number.

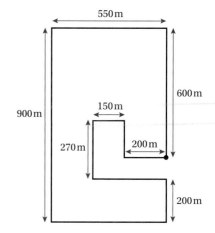

Jamie goes to the local cake shop for the office tea break orders.

One day Jamie bought four cups of tea and six cupcakes. That order cost £9.20.

Another day Jamie bought five cups of tea and two cupcakes. That came to a total of £7.10.

a Write an equation for Jamie's first visit to the shop.

b Write an equation for Jamie's second visit to the shop.

c Solve the equations and find the price of one cupcake and one cup of tea.

Tip
Let x represent the cost of a cup of tea and y represent the cost of a cupcake.

Alison is planning to make a patchwork quilt for her niece. She has chosen to include the pattern on the right as part of her design. The centre piece of this pattern is a regular hexagon.

a Show that Alison cannot produce this pattern by using regular pentagons on her quilt.

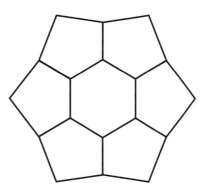

It would be much easier if Alison could create a pattern made up of regular shapes.

b She still wants to use a regular hexagon for the centre piece. Can she use any sort of regular polygon for the 'petals'?

c If she wanted to use regular pentagons for the 'petals', which regular polygon would she need in the centre?

Tip
What do you know about a regular hexagon? What angles can you work out? What about a regular pentagon?

Tip
How might it be useful to know about interior and exterior angles in this problem?

Adding lines is a strategy that works for some geometry problems. Sometimes an extra line is very helpful. On other occasions it turns out to be useless. How can you tell which type of line to use? Let's work through an example problem.

> In the diagram below, two parallel lines are shown. Work out the size of angle α.

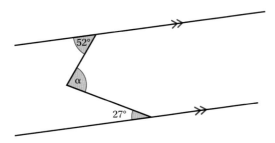

There are several different ways to solve this problem. Here are three of them, all of which involve adding extra lines to the diagram.

Solution 1

Add a line parallel to the other two lines and that passes through the angle you want to work out:

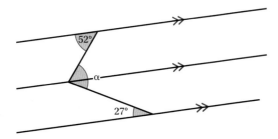

Could this help you?

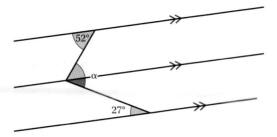

The angle shown in red is equal to 27°. Can you explain why?

What is the other part of angle α equal to? What is angle α?

Solution 2

Add a line that is perpendicular to the parallel lines and passes through the point of the angle, as shown in the next diagram.

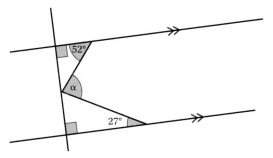

You now have two triangles. In those triangles you know two of the angles, so you can work out the third one. Do that now, remembering to mark the angles on the diagram. Here you use the strategy from Chapter 2 and advice from Chapter 1 to annotate a diagram by adding new information when you work it out.

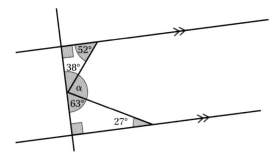

In the middle of this diagram there is a straight line, so now you can work out the missing angle α.

Solution 3

Add a line that is perpendicular to the parallel lines and passes through the point of the 27° angle as shown in the diagram below.

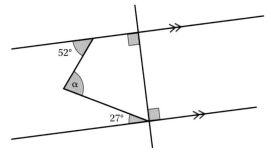

You can see a quadrilateral in the middle of the diagram. You can also 'see' what to do to solve the problem: You can work out three of the angles in the quadrilateral and you know that all of the angles add up to 360°.

Let's go back to the question we posed at the beginning: How can you tell which type of line to use?

The short answer is that you can't. There are lots of different lines you could have drawn on this diagram that wouldn't have helped you. For example, the line in the diagram below is not helpful.

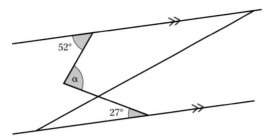

A line that is 'special' in some way is more likely to be helpful.

Try using lines that:

- are parallel to other lines
- are perpendicular to other lines
- are lines of symmetry
- join up two points
- join midpoints of sides of shapes.

Here is another case where extra lines make a question easier to answer.

The perimeter of the shape on the right is 34. Work out x.

You could work out the lengths of the other sides, but instead you could put two extra lines on the diagram.

Can you see why the perimeter of the rectangle is the same as the perimeter of the original shape?

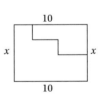

The perimeter is $x + 10 + x + 10$, which equals 34.

This means $x = 7$.

The following problems may be solved using more than one method; however, the worked solutions provided at the back of this book are based on the method introduced above.

An ant walks from vertex *A* to vertex *G*, always moving along the edges of the cuboid.

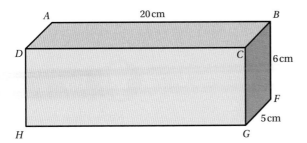

a What distance does the ant walk if it goes from *A* to *D* to *H* to *G*?

b What distance does the ant walk if it goes via *E*, the hidden vertex of the cuboid?

c Walking only on the edges, what is the shortest distance the ant could walk if it started at vertex *B* and returned to *B* without walking on any edge twice?

d Investigate the longest distance the ant could walk if it went from vertex *B* to *H* and back to *B* without travelling along the same edge more than once.

ABCD is a rectangle. $\overrightarrow{AB}$ is **a** and $\overrightarrow{BC}$ is **b**.

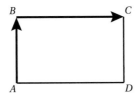

Is $\overrightarrow{AC}$ is the same as $\overrightarrow{DB}$? Explain your answer.

Liz looks up at the clock on her wall. She is disappointed that it is not yet 5 pm, which is the time she can go home.

a   Through how many degrees must the minute hand of the clock turn before Liz can leave work?

b   Through what angle must the hour hand turn before Liz can leave?

Tip

Remember that on a clock, the hour hand moves continuously, just like the minute hand. What angle does each hand turn through in one hour?

Gerry has a swimming pool at his holiday home. He wants to put a short fence around the pool, to prevent small children falling in.

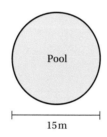

Pool

15 m

Tip

Draw good diagrams!

He wants the fence to surround the pool, shown in the diagram above, completely and at a distance of 1 m from its edge.

a   Calculate the length of fencing that Gerry will need to buy. Give your answer correct to 3 significant figures.

Ian needs to build a fence around his pool, but it is a different shape from Gerry's, as shown in the diagram below. Ian would like to build his fence at a distance of 1.5 m from the edge of his pool.

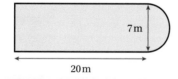

7 m

20 m

b   Will Ian need more fencing than Gerry? Explain your answer.

A window cleaner has a ladder made of three sections. Its first section is the longest, the second section is 60 cm shorter and the third section is 60 cm shorter than the second one.

The total length of the ladder is 5.1 m.

How long is each section?

Quadrilateral *ABCD* is drawn on this coordinate grid.

Quadrilateral *EFGH* is mathematically similar to *ABCD*.

Length *AB* corresponds to length *EF*, as shown on the grid.

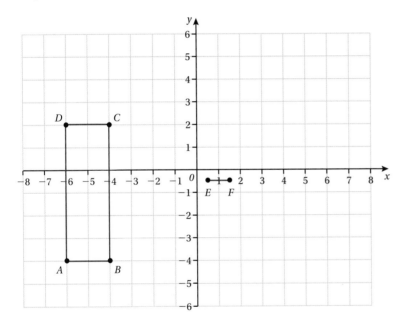

What are the coordinates of points *G* and *H*?

Use trigonometry to show that the two right-angled triangles in the diagram below have the same area.

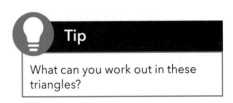

Tip

What can you work out in these triangles?

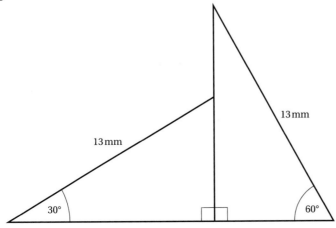

8

Show how the shape on the right could be divided up:

a To create **three** congruent shapes.

b To create **four** congruent shapes.

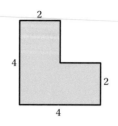

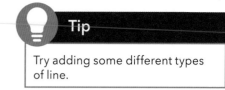

Tip

Try adding some different types of line.

9

Lorna is going to Glasgow for a fortnight. She is travelling from London and there are a couple of different options.

Lorna can go by coach direct from London to Glasgow. Alternatively, she can go by train with a change in Birmingham and a wait of 1 hour 45 minutes.

The distance from London to Glasgow is 650 km.

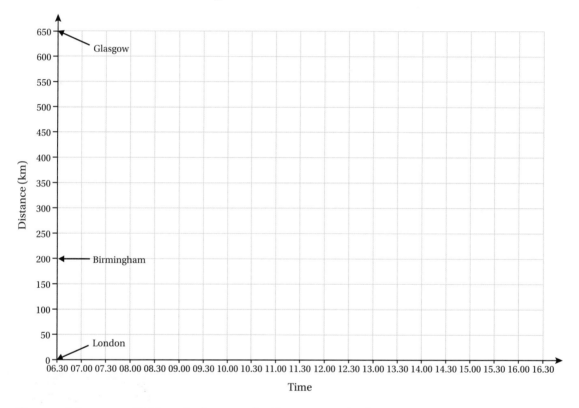

The coach leaves at 06.30 and takes exactly 8 hours to arrive in Glasgow.

If Lorna goes by train she would leave London at 07.00 and arrive in Birmingham at 08.40.

The train journey from Birmingham to Glasgow should then take 4 hours and 15 minutes.

a What is the average speed for the coach journey?

b What is the average speed for the train journey?

The perimeter of the shape shown on the right is 2.28 km.

Calculate the value of *a*. Give your answer in kilometres.

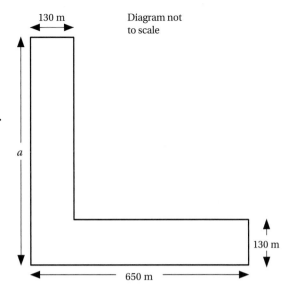

130 m

Diagram not to scale

a

130 m

650 m

Tip

Remember: 1 km = 1000 m. You could add more information to the diagram as you work it out.

Students taking part in a mathematical challenge are shown the diagram on the right.

They are asked: '**What proportion of the outer triangle is coloured purple?**'

After some thought the teams hand in their answer:

Team **A**: 24 cm²

Team **B**: $\frac{3}{4}$

Team **C**: $\left(\frac{3}{4}\right)^2$

Team **D**: 0.5625

The question is marked out of 4 marks. How many marks would you award each team? Justify your decisions.

A pizza restaurant offers two styles of pizza: classic and rustic.
The classic pizza is a standard circular pizza. The rustic pizza is
rectangular with semicircular ends, as shown in the diagram below.

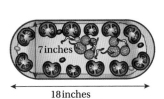

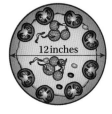

Rustic

Classic

The restaurant charges more for the rustic pizza, but do you actually
get more for your money?

Tip

Remember to justify your answer,
using numbers and words. Your
conclusions must be convincing.

ABCDEF is a regular hexagon.

A has coordinates (2, 1).

The column vector $\overrightarrow{AB} = \begin{pmatrix} 0 \\ 2 \end{pmatrix}$.

a What is the column vector for $\overrightarrow{DE}$?

The coordinates of *C* are $(2 + \sqrt{3}, 4)$.

b What is the column vector for $\overrightarrow{BC}$?

c What is the column vector for $\overrightarrow{FC}$?

d What is the column vector for $\overrightarrow{AE}$?

e What is the column vector for $\overrightarrow{AC}$?

f What is the column vector for $\overrightarrow{EF}$?

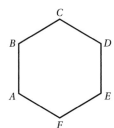

The graphs of two quadratic equations are shown below.

The blue parabola is symmetrical about the line $x = 2$ and has roots at A and B.

The blue parabola is reflected in the x-axis to create the red parabola. The red parabola has roots at C and D.

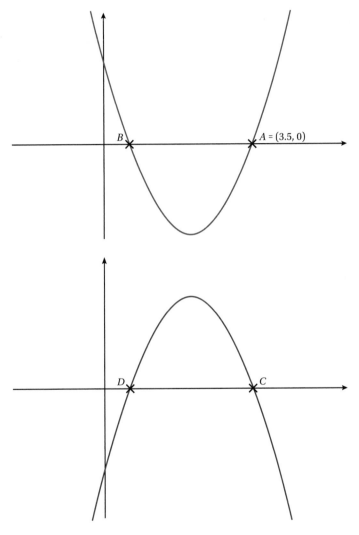

Work out the coordinates of points B, C and D.

Mandeep is investigating patterns in circles. He draws eight dots equally spaced around a circle.

He draws a triangle by connecting three of the dots. The line *AC* passes through the centre of the circle, *O*.

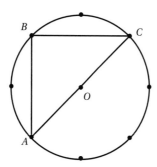

a Use this image to show that ∠*ABC* is a right angle.

He draws another triangle by connecting a different set of three dots. The line *AC* still passes through the centre of the circle.

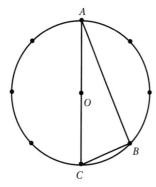

b Is ∠*ABC* still a right angle?

Mandeep draws another circle with 10 dots equally spaced around its circumference. Again, he draws a triangle by connecting three of these dots. The line *AC* passes through the centre of the circle.

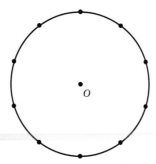

c Show that for a triangle of your choice, meeting these conditions, the sum of angle *BAC* and angle *BCA* is still 90°.

Charlie's house has two floors connected by a staircase. The vertical distance between the two floors is 3.6 m. Each step of the staircase is 18 cm high and 28 cm deep.

Tip

The diagram is a useful start but is missing some important lines.

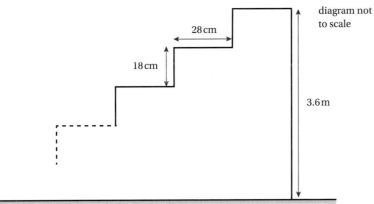

diagram not to scale

28 cm

18 cm

3.6 m

a How many steps are there?

b How long will the banister rail be?

Students on a field trip are shown a clever trick to estimate the height of a tall tree. They point to the tree with their arm at an angle of approximately 45° and look along it. They then walk backwards until their arm is pointing to the top of the tree.

The distance from the student to the tree trunk will then be approximately the same as the height of the tree.

a Explain why this method gives a rough idea of the height of the tree.

Two students, Kelly and Guy, try this out. Guy ends up standing 3 m in front of Kelly.

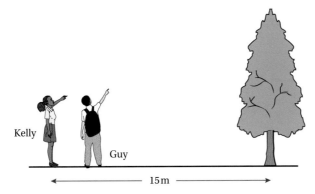

Kelly

Guy

15 m

b If Kelly's angle is exactly 45°, at what angle must Guy be holding his arm?

Sometimes there is a problem that is just too complicated to solve immediately. One way to deal with this is to make the problem simpler. This won't directly tell you the answer because it will be a slightly different problem, but it might give you a starting point. Here's an example.

> George climbs a staircase that has 10 steps. He can go from one step to the next one (1-step), or miss out a step and go up two at once (2-step). How many different ways can he go up the stairs?

You could draw a diagram, but you will quickly produce a picture with too many lines.

You could also write down the different possibilities, using 1 to stand for '1-step' and 2 to stand for '2-step'.

So:

   1111111111

   1211212

   22222

   etc

But there are too many possibilities and it just looks too hard.

You could make the problem simpler. Let's make it very simple indeed. Imagine that George wants to climb a flight of stairs that has 1 step. This is easy: 1 way (if he tries to do a 2-step he will only actually go up 1 step). Now try 2 steps. There are 2 ways. The diagram below shows the working.

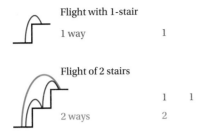

Flight with 1-stair

1 way   1

Flight of 2 stairs

                                    1   1

2 ways   2

You could now look at the pattern of answers in the table below to see if that will help.

Number of steps	Number of ways of climbing them
1	1
2	2
3	3
4	5
5	8

Do you recognise the number sequence in the second column?

1, 2, 3, 5, 8 is part of the Fibonacci Sequence, where you add the two previous numbers to get the next one. $1 + 2 = 3$, $2 + 3 = 5$, $3 + 5 = 8$. If this is the right sequence then the next one will be $5 + 8 = 13$. You don't want to draw this out, so instead think about why this might be sensible.

When you look at the numbers written next to each flight of stairs you can see some similarities.

Here are the routes up 5 steps:	**If you remove the final number you get this sequence:**	
11111	1111	
2111	211	
221	22	
212	21	
1211	121	
122	12	
1112	111	
1121	112	

← and these are the ways of climbing 3 and 4 steps!

Why does that make sense?

Well, if you want to climb 5 steps, you could go up 4 steps and then do a 1-step to get to the top. So you need all of the ways of climbing 4 steps with a 1 at the end. Alternatively, you can get to step 3 and then do a 2-step to get to the top, so you need all of the ways of climbing 3 steps with a 2 after them. This means you really are adding the previous two numbers together.

To climb 10 steps you need to continue the sequence: 1, 2, 3, 5, 8, 13, 21, 34, 55, 89. So there are 89 ways to climb the stairs.

Here, simplifying the problem meant you could get started and see what was going on.

Let's look at another example problem.

> What is the smallest number that can be divided (with no remainder) by all of the numbers from 1 to 12?

What do you know already?

Clearly the number will have to end with a zero (to make it divisible by 10). It will have to be even so it is divisible by 2 (but if it ends with a zero then that is already the case).

One strategy that might be useful is to make the problem simpler:

What is the smallest number that can be divided by all numbers from 1 to 3?

If you do $2 \times 3 = 6$ then you know that 6 can be divided by 1, 2 and 3. Is it the smallest number? Yes.

What is the smallest number that can be divided by all numbers from 1 to 4?

If you do $2 \times 3 \times 4 = 24$ then you know that can be divided by 1, 2, 3 and 4. But there is a smaller number that works. 12 can be divided by 1, 2, 3 and 4. Why didn't $2 \times 3 \times 4$ give you the right answer? To make the number divisible by 4 you didn't need to multiply the previous answer by 4, because there was already a 2 involved. If you had just multiplied the previous answer by 2 that would have given you a number divisible by 4.

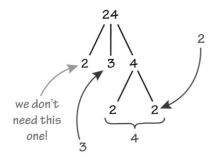 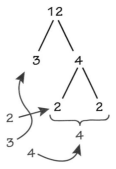

Therefore the answer is $2 \times 3 \times 2 = 12$.

Do you notice that these numbers are prime numbers?

Try the next one:

What is the smallest number that can be divided by all numbers from 1 to 5?

You currently have $2 \times 3 \times 2$, which is not helpful if you want it to be divisible by 5. The trick that you used with 4 (splitting it into 2×2) won't work here because 5 is a prime number. To make it a multiple of 5 you will need to multiply by 5, giving you $2 \times 3 \times 2 \times 5 = 60$.

You can see that the next one is easy.

What is the smallest number that can be divided by all numbers from 1 to 6?

60 is obviously already divisible by 6, and you can see that in the numbers because 2 × 3 is in there. 2 × 3 × 2 × 5 is divisible by all numbers from 1 to 6.

To make the smallest number divisible by 7 we need to include a 7, because 7 is a prime number.

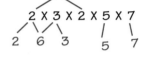

To make it divisible by 7 you therefore need to have 2 × 3 × 2 × 5 × 7.

To make it divisible by 8 you only need an extra 2 because it is already divisible by 4, and to make it divisible by 9 you need an extra 3.

You know it is already divisible by 10 (because it ends with a zero).

11 is a prime number so you need to have 2 × 3 × 2 × 5 × 7 × 2 × 3 × 11.

The first three numbers in this product make 12 (2 × 3 × 2) so it is divisible by 12.

Your final answer is therefore: 2 × 3 × 2 × 5 × 7 × 2 × 3 × 11 = 27 720.

The following problems may be solved using more than one method; however, the worked solutions provided at the back of this book are based on the method introduced above.

Tip

There are other ways to solve this problem, such as realising that the question is really the same as asking for the lowest common multiple of the numbers 1 to 12.

Simon and Jamie are playing a game of 'Guess the number'.

Jamie says: 'If I multiply my number by 7 and then subtract 10, my final answer is 25.'

a What is Jamie's number?

Simon takes his turn. 'If I add 9 to my number then divide by 4, my final answer is 5.'

b What is Simon's number?

Tip

Working backwards from the answers should lead to the starting value.

Farmer Jones is constructing pig runs for his prize pigs. He is making them hexagonal in shape.

The hexagons will be regular and each side will be made of three panels, each of exactly the same length. Farmer Jones wants the pens each to have a perimeter of 10.8 m.

What will be the length, in metres, of each panel?

Tip

Write the equation that describes the perimeter of the pen.

Frances has 40 cubes to pack into a box. Each cube has sides of 5 cm.

a Sketch a box that will hold all the cubes without any spaces.

b Write the dimensions of the box on your diagram.

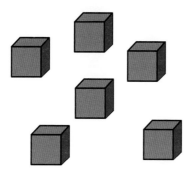

 Consider each of the calculations below. Without using a calculator, decide if they have an even result.

a $4^3 + 3^4 = ?$

b $6^7 + 3^7 = ?$

Tip

What type of number (odd or even) is 4^3?
What about 3^4?

5

Ahmed buys a piece of wood measuring 12 cm by 5 cm by 1 m for £5.

He uses the piece of wood to make 40 door wedges like the one in the diagram below.

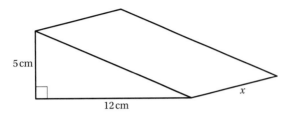

5 cm

12 cm

x

a What is the width x, in cm, of the wedges?

b What is the lowest price Ahmed could sell the wedges for to make at least £30 profit?

6

A cinema offers discounted tickets on Thursdays.

Normal ticket prices

Adult: £7.60   Child: £3.40

Thursday ticket prices

Adult: £7.00   Child: £2.95

The cinema has 150 seats.

Calculate the percentage difference in takings on a Thursday, compared with other days, in the following situations:

a The cinema is completely filled with adults.

b The cinema is completely filled with children.

c The cinema is filled with families (in the ratio of 1 adult : 1 child).

7

Helen drives to work every day. On her journey there is a level crossing, a set of traffic lights and a roundabout. At each of these she must either stop or be allowed to continue.

The probability of stopping at the level crossing is $\frac{1}{10}$.

The probability of stopping at the lights is $\frac{1}{4}$.

The probability of stopping at the roundabout is $\frac{2}{3}$.

What is the probability that on Helen's next journey to work she does not have to stop at any of them?

Tip

What happens if there is only the level crossing? Is there a diagram that would help with this? Then you could introduce the traffic lights too.

Calculate the missing length on the trapezium.

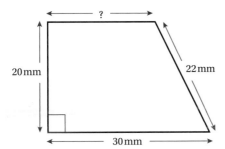

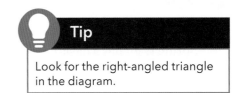

Tip

Look for the right-angled triangle in the diagram.

Two almost identical logos are shown in the diagram below. Both show a square of 10 cm with a second square tilted inside it.

Tip

How could you work out the lengths of one of the red lines?

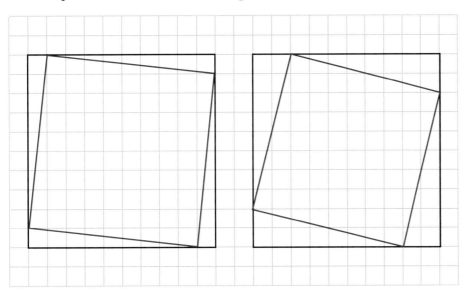

Prove that the total (ie red and black) line lengths are shorter in the right-hand square.

Trevor is investigating the price of hiring a bouncy castle.

Spring High has a basic charge of £18, plus £1.80 for every hour.

Castle Jump has a basic charge of £20, plus £1.30 per hour.

Trevor is certain he won't need the castle for any longer than 5 hours.

a Copy the axes provided and plot a graph to show the charges for Spring High.

b Using your graph, find the price Spring High would charge Trevor to have the bouncy castle from 1 pm until 6 pm.

c On the same axes, plot a graph for Castle Jump's charges.

d For approximately what length of time would the charge be the same from both companies?

Tip

To start your graphs, plot how much it would cost to have the bouncy castle for 0 hours.
Then work out how much it would cost for 1 hour.

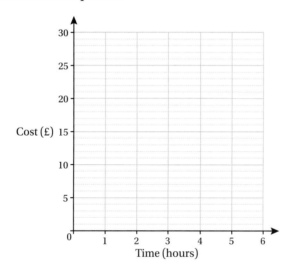

Is it possible for you to count out loud from one to a million in your lifetime?

Tip

To answer this question you will need to make estimates based on various assumptions. You should also round your answers to an appropriate degree of accuracy. You might like to consider how long it takes you to count from one to ten, and how long it takes you to count (out loud) much longer numbers.

Anna knows that she can create a heart shape from a triangle and two semicircles. She makes a Valentine's card by cutting a heart shape out of a piece of card, as shown below.

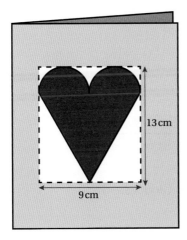

What area has Anna removed from the white area to make her card? Give your answer correct to 3 significant figures.

Larry's aunt gives Larry £40 000 to put into a compound interest savings account.

ABC Bank is offering 8% compound interest on your money if you invest more than £30 000 and the money remains in the bank for at least ten years.

Larry's aunt tells him that his money will more than double if he invests his money for ten years.

a Is Larry's aunt correct?

b How much will Larry have in his account at the end of ten years?

Larry's aunt decides to invest some of her own money for ten years. She wants to make a profit and have a total of at least £75 000 at the end of the ten-year period.

c What is the smallest amount (to the nearest £1000) Larry's aunt must invest to have at least £75 000 at the end of ten years?

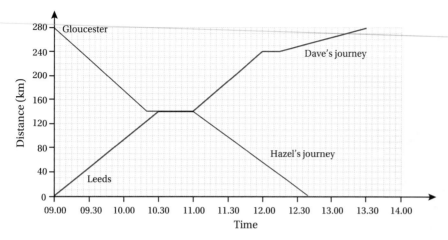

Dave makes the 280 km motorway journey from Leeds to Gloucester by car, and his travel graph is shown above.

Hazel travels from Gloucester to Leeds on the same day but on a motorcycle.

Hazel's travel graph is also shown on the diagram.

Both Dave and Hazel set out on their journeys at 09.00.

a What was Dave's speed for the first 140 km?

b What was Hazel's speed for the first stage of her journey?

c How long did Hazel have to wait before Dave arrived at the service station where they were meeting for coffee?

d Dave got caught up in a traffic jam following an accident just outside of Gloucester. What time was this?

e How long did Dave's journey take? What was his average speed?

f How long did Hazel's journey take? What was her average speed?

g Should either of them receive a speeding ticket for any stage of their journeys?

Tip

In UK the national speed on motorways is 70 miles per hour. To convert kilometres to miles, divide by 8 and multiply by 5.

Making changes to the problem is another strategy that works particularly well with some geometric problems. This time you won't necessarily simplify the problem (as you did in the previous chapter) but you could adjust it in a way that doesn't change its important features. This might allow you to see what is going on.

> In this diagram *AB* is the diameter of the circle, *C* lies on the circumference and *O* is the centre of the circle. What is the relationship between the area of triangle *OAC* and triangle *OBC*? Explain your answer.

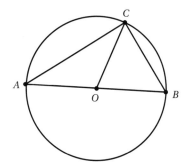

The question asks: 'What is the relationship?' What could that mean? Perhaps one is double the other? Maybe they are the same?

In this diagram it looks as if the areas might be the same. Can you provide evidence to convince yourself that this is the case?

After that, can you convince someone else that this is the case?

The key points are:

- there is a circle
- *AB* is the diameter of the circle
- *O* is the centre of the circle and
- points *A*, *B* and *C* are on the circle.

All of this must stay true. You might be able to move some of the points so the answer is obvious. There doesn't seem to be anything special about the placing of point *C*, so it might be acceptable for you to move the points around. It wouldn't be acceptable for you to move *C* off the circle, though, because that would change the situation.

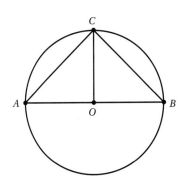

The diagram on the right looks good. *C* has moved so that it is halfway between *A* and *B* but still on the circle. There is now a line of symmetry in the diagram and the two triangles are clearly equal.

Here is another special case.

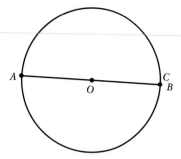

C has moved so that it is on top of point *B*. This time the two triangles both have zero area, so they are the same.

The idea that the two areas are the same is looking likely.

How do you work out the area of a triangle?

It is half of the base multiplied by the perpendicular height (the dashed line in the diagram below).

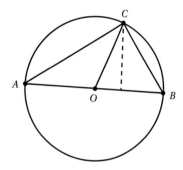

In the right-hand triangle, the area is the radius of the circle (*OB*) multiplied by the dashed line (the perpendicular height), divided by two.

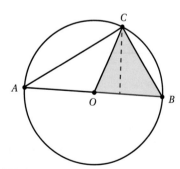

In the left-hand triangle, the area is the radius of the circle (*AO*) multiplied by the perpendicular height, divided by two. But what is the perpendicular height for the left-hand triangle? It is actually the dashed line.

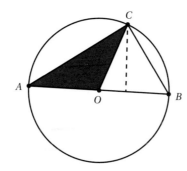

So they do have the same area and you can explain why.

This is an example where adding an extra line can help us, see Chapter 3. A good diagram is also important here, see Chapter 1.

So, what sort of changes might be useful? Try:

- moving points around (but preserving the initial situation)
- creating a special situation (e.g. a line of symmetry)
- moving points to extreme positions.

Here is another problem.

> Triangular numbers can be shown as stacks of squares like this:
>
> There are 10 squares, so 10 is a triangular number.
>
> The triangular numbers are 1, 3, 6, 10, 15, 21, 28, etc.
>
> Show that if you add two adjacent triangular numbers you always get a square number.

You could try this out: $1 + 3 = 4$ $3 + 6 = 9$ $15 + 21 = 36$

This looks good, but how do you know it will always be true?

If you draw a square around a triangular number what happens?

The empty space looks interesting. Now push the squares over to the side:

The red part is a triangular number and the white part is the previous triangular number!

The following problems may be solved using more than one method; however, the worked solutions provided at the back of this book are based on the method introduced above.

What is the **same** and what's **different** about the pairs of calculations below?

a $\frac{1}{3} + 1$ and $1 + \frac{1}{3}$

b $1 - \frac{1}{3}$ and $\frac{1}{3} - 1$

Three pairs of fractions are shown below. In each case the smaller fraction is on the left-hand side.

i $\frac{1}{4} < \frac{1}{2}$ **ii** $\frac{2}{6} < \frac{4}{10}$ **iii** $\frac{5}{8} < \frac{5}{7}$

How could you change one of the fractions in each pair so that the smaller fraction was on the right-hand side?

Describe the mathematical process that will change the fraction in each case.

Tip

Try to be specific about how you have changed a fraction.
- Have you multiplied or divided it by something? If so, by what?
- Have you added something? If so, what have you added?
- Have you subtracted something? If so, what have you subtracted?

Alina is asked to write down five different fractions in ascending order.

She thinks carefully and then writes:

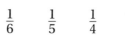
$$\frac{1}{6} \qquad \frac{1}{5} \qquad \frac{1}{4} \qquad \frac{1}{3} \qquad \frac{1}{2}$$

a Suggest another set of fractions that Alina could have written.

b Suggest another set of fractions where none has a numerator of 1.

c Suggest a final set of fractions all of which have greater numerators than denominators.

Tip

There are lots of ways to do this. One way is to change the original set of fractions.

$23.64 \times 805 = 1903.02$

How can you tell that this statement is incorrect?

Tip

How could you change the question to make it obvious that there is a mistake?

Which is bigger?

a $400\,\text{g} + 400\,\text{mg}$ or $0.5\,\text{kg} - 90\,\text{g}$

b $0.1\,\text{km} + 150\,\text{cm}$ or $110\,\text{m} - 900\,\text{cm}$

c 0.75 hours $+ 600$ seconds or 50 minutes $+ 0.1$ hours

Tip

Remember that to compare quantities, they need to be measured in the same units.

Felix likes to grow flowers. He bought some lily bulbs. The lilies will be white, purple or red in colour.

The probability of the first lily to flower being red is $\frac{1}{5}$. The probability of the first lily to flower being purple is 0.7.

a What is the probability that the first lily to flower will be white?

b If Felix bought 140 lily bulbs, how many of them are likely to produce purple flowers?

Unfortunately $\frac{1}{7}$ of the 140 bulbs fail to grow.

c How many of the remainder would you expect to have red flowers?

Four snails have a race.

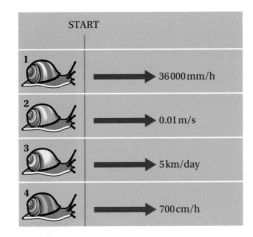

START
1 — 36 000 mm/h
2 — 0.01 m/s
3 — 5 km/day
4 — 700 cm/h

Tip

In order to compare the snails you will need to convert their speeds into the same units.

Assuming that the snails move at a constant speed to the finish line, which one will get there first?

This is the flag of the Seychelles (a group of islands off the east coast of Africa).

The top and the right-hand side are both divided into thirds.

Is the area of the white triangle bigger, smaller or the same as the area of the blue triangle? Explain your answer.

9

Mei chooses three consecutive integers and adds them together.
5 + 6 + 7 = 18

She notices that 18 is also the result of 6 × 3.

Mei selects another set of three numbers and adds them together.
2 + 3 + 4 = 9

She notices that 9 is also the result of 3 × 3.

It looks like the sum of three consecutive numbers is the same as the middle number multiplied by three.

a Is this always true?

b Can you find a rule for adding four consecutive integers?

c How might you extend your rule to add five or more consecutive integers?

10

Lois is moving house. She has 600 CDs. Each CD case measures 142 mm × 125 mm × 10 mm.

a How many of her CDs can she pack into the box on the right?

b How many more boxes will she need to be able to transport all her CDs?

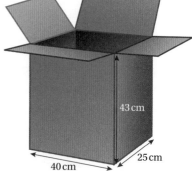

43 cm

40 cm

25 cm

11

Daisy draws a shape on a coordinate grid as shown in the diagram below.

a Daisy notices that the centre of her shape (marked with the black dot on the diagram) lies on the line $x = -5$. How could Daisy translate her shape so that its centre remains on the line $x = -5$?

b Daisy's shape also lies on the line $y = x$. How could she translate her shape so that its centre remains on the line $y = x$?

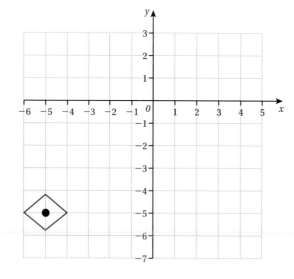

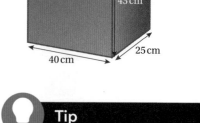

Tip

Remember to use vector notation to describe a particular translation.
Is there more than one solution to each part of this question? If so, can you write your answers in a more general way (using words or mathematical notation)?

Melissa is starting a business. She has designed the logo shown below. It is based on an isosceles triangle with a semicircle on each edge.

Calculate the perimeter of Melissa's logo.

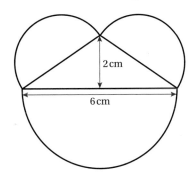

Tip

Remember, you can use Pythagoras' theorem to calculate missing lengths in right-angled triangles.

Mikey is asked to investigate what happens when a shape is reflected in two perpendicular mirror lines in turn.

He draws the following picture and makes the observation: 'Ah! It's just the same as a translation of the original shape.'

Tip

'Perpendicular' means that the mirror lines are at right angles (90°) to each other.

Why did Mikey choose his pair of mirror lines to be the x and y axes? Are there other pairs that he could have chosen?

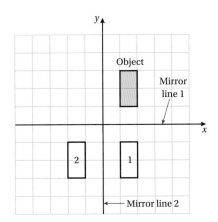

Mikey's teacher looks at his work and asks: 'Are you sure?'

a Suggest how Mikey could investigate this.

b By considering the starting point shown in the diagram below, decide whether or not you agree with Mikey's first idea.

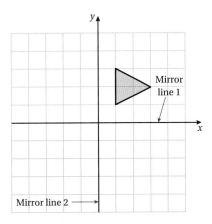

As you work through more problem-solving questions, you are likely to find problems similar to ones you have worked on before. Even if they are not identical some of the ideas you used in earlier problems might help. Here is an example.

> Multiply two consecutive even numbers. Do you always get a multiple of 8? Justify your answer.

You could start by trying a few to see if it appears to be true (but this won't justify or prove it):

$2 \times 4 = 8$ $4 \times 6 = 24$

$6 \times 8 = 48$ $10 \times 12 = 120$

All of these are multiples of 8. It is looking good so far (but you haven't justified it).

You could approach this problem by looking at factors, or you could use some algebra.

What can you use for the two numbers? If you call them a and b that doesn't include the idea that they are **even** numbers. If you call them $2a$ and $2b$ that could help. You need a and b to be consecutive whole numbers. This tells us that either a or b is even. If you do $2a \times 2b$ you get $4ab$, but one of a and b is even so the whole thing must be a multiple of 8.

Here is a slightly more formal way to do the same thing, using just a single letter. If the first even number is $2a$ then you can call the next one $2a + 2$. When you multiply these you get $2a(2a + 2)$. This is equal to $4a^2 + 4a$, which is $4a(a + 1)$.

Let's look at $4a(a + 1)$.

If a is odd then $a + 1$ is even and you have $4 \times \text{odd} \times \text{even}$, which is a multiple of 8 (because 4 multiplied by an even number is a multiple of 8). If $a + 1$ is odd then a is even and you have $4 \times \text{even} \times \text{odd}$, which is a multiple of 8.

So the whole thing is a multiple of 8.

Here is another example.

> Choose any three consecutive positive integers. Add them together. Is the answer always a multiple of 3? Is the answer always a multiple of 6? Explain your answer.

This problem is similar to the previous one, so you could use similar techniques. First, try a few numbers just to get a feel for what is going on. Then use some algebra and try to create an expression to describe what is happening.

$1 + 2 + 3 = 6$ This is a multiple of 3 and also a multiple of 6.

$2 + 3 + 4 = 9$ This is a multiple of 3 but not a multiple of 6.

You have already shown that the answer is **not** always a multiple of 6 because you have found one that doesn't work.

Using algebra, you could call the first number a. The next number will therefore be $a + 1$ and the one after that will be $a + 2$. This is similar to what you did in the previous example so you are using the experience you gained doing that question.

When you add these together you get $a + a + 1 + a + 2$, which equals $3a + 3$. To show that this is clearly divisible by 3 you could factorise: $3(a + 1)$, to show that you have an integer $(a + 1)$ multiplied by 3.

If you call the middle number n then it happens to be even easier. The three numbers are: $n - 1$, n, $n + 1$, and adding these gives $3n$. Note that you didn't use three different letters to describe the numbers. This is often useful.

The following problems may be solved using more than one method; however, the worked solutions provided at the back of this book are based on the method introduced above.

For each pair of decimal numbers below decide which is smaller. Explain how you know in each case.

a 1.099 and 1.308   **b** 0.5 and 0.500

c 1.7 and 1.534

> **Tip**
>
> This is not really problem solving, but the difficult part here might be explaining how you know.

The perimeter of this isosceles triangle is 41 cm.

What are the lengths of the three sides?

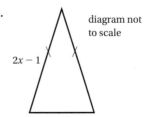

diagram not to scale

$2x - 1$

$x + 3$

> **Tip**
>
> Can you write the perimeter using algebra? What is this algebra equal to?

Two handprints are shown in the diagram below.

Approximately how many times bigger is handprint A than handprint B?

Tip

This is a question about area. The handprints have been shown on a square grid. How many different ways could you use this to estimate the area of each handprint? Which method is better for this particular question?

Jeremy makes lemonade using $2.5\,l$ of water, $500\,ml$ of concentrated sugar solution and $750\,ml$ of lemon juice.

a Express these quantities as a ratio.

b How many litres of lemonade does Jeremy make?

This lemonade is too sweet, so Jeremy makes another batch using half the amount of sugar solution but the same quantities of the other ingredients.

c Express Jeremy's quantities as a ratio.

d How much lemonade did Jeremy make with his new recipe?

Tip

Let the water be 2500 parts.

A fair six-sided dice is rolled. What is the probability of getting a:

a multiple of 2

b square number

c number greater than 4

d prime number

e 9?

Tip

Do you remember doing probability in lessons? Have you also used multiples, primes and squares in the past? Can you combine these topics?

Razi has taken up golf and often goes to the golf range. He notices that in every bucket of 30 balls he gets four yellow balls.

a Razi randomly picks a ball from the bucket. What is the probability that the first ball Razi uses is a yellow ball?

One morning, Razi uses five buckets of balls.

b How many of the balls Razi uses are yellow?

c What is the probability that Razi's furthest shot that day is with a yellow ball? Simplify your answer.

The population of the Earth is approximately 7 billion (to the nearest billion).

a What is the smallest the population could be?

b What is the largest the population could be?

c If the population of the Earth is p, write down an inequality to represent the range of values that it could take.

 Tip

What's the difference between the greatest possible number of people and the smallest possible number of people? You should use your answers to parts **a** and **b** to help you.

1 billion = 1 000 000 000. This means that 7 billion is 7 000 000 000 people.

d By how many people could the population vary?

Paul wants to buy a mixture of jam and iced doughnuts.

Iced doughnuts cost 15p more than jam doughnuts.

a A jam doughnut costs t pence. Write an expression for the price of an iced doughnut.

Paul buys 3 jam doughnuts and 5 iced doughnuts. The total cost is £11.95.

b How much does it cost to buy six of each type of doughnut?

The instructions for cooking poultry are: '50 minutes per kg plus an additional 30 minutes.'

For Christmas, Fergus needs to cook a 3 kg chicken and a 7.5 kg turkey.

He wants both birds to be ready at the same time. He needs 20 minutes to carve and prepare the serving dishes, once they are taken out of the oven. He wants to serve lunch at 1.00 pm on Christmas Day.

a How long will the turkey be in the oven by itself before being joined by the chicken?

b Find a formula to find the time taken, t minutes, to cook a chicken weighing m kg.

For New Year's Day, Fergus plans to cook a goose. This goose will take 5 hours and 5 minutes to cook.

c How much does the goose weigh?

d If Fergus plans to have a late lunch at 2.30 pm on New Year's Day, what is the latest time he can put the goose in the oven?

The final speed v of a car is given by the formula $v = u + at$ where u is the initial speed, a is the acceleration and t is the time.

a Find the final speed of a car where $u = 22$ m/s, $t = 30$ seconds and $a = 0.4$ m/s^2.

b A car started from rest. Its final speed is 50 m/s and the acceleration was 0.2 m/s^2. For how long was the car accelerating?

c If a car accelerates for 15 seconds at 2.5 m/s^2, and its final speed is 90 m/s, what was its initial speed?

Nick has a poster on the wall in his office.

a If Nick actually worked in this way, how long would he work on a Friday?

b How much longer would Nick work for on a Wednesday compared with a Monday?

Bernard has a similar poster.

c Why can't you tell for certain who works longer on a Tuesday?

> **ALWAYS GIVE 100% AT WORK**
>
> 12% MONDAY
> 23% TUESDAY
> 40% WEDNESDAY
> 20% THURSDAY
> 5% FRIDAY

Nick's poster

> **ALWAYS GIVE 100% AT WORK**
>
> 14% MONDAY
> 18% TUESDAY
> 29% WEDNESDAY
> 36% THURSDAY
> 3% FRIDAY

Bernard's poster

Tip

You will need to decide how long a working day is. What is its usual length?

Twenty years ago Lady Sophia wrote her will. She had a son, twin daughters and a poodle. Lady Sophia's house and possessions (her estate) were valued at £5 000 000.

Lady Sophia had decided to leave half of her estate to her son, a third to her daughters to be shared equally between them, and to give the rest to the local pet rescue centre.

a What fraction of the estate would the pet rescue centre have received?

b Express these fractions as a ratio in the order of son : daughter : daughter : pet rescue centre.

c To the nearest thousand pounds, how much would each daughter have received?

Twenty years later Lady Sophia has spent $\frac{2}{5}$ of her money. She writes a new will stating that her three children should each have $\frac{1}{4}$ of her estate. The rest is to be shared equally between her five grandchildren. Lady Sophia is no longer leaving any money to the pet rescue centre.

d How much will each child inherit?

e How much will each grandchild inherit?

Under the second will Lady Sophia's son will inherit a different amount to the first.

f Express the two amounts for the son as a ratio.

A butcher always uses the same mix of minced chicken, minced turkey and herbs in his sausages.

For every 4 kg of turkey he adds 7 kg of chicken and 250 g of herbs.

a If the butcher uses 6 kg of minced turkey, how much minced chicken does he require?

b How many grams of herbs does he need?

c How much turkey would the butcher need if he used 28 kg of chicken?

d Express the ingredients (herbs : turkey : chicken) in the form of $1 : m : n$.

At an MK Dons home match against Chelsea, MK Dons had 25 200 supporters in the stadium.

The ratio of home to away supporters was 21 : 4.

a How many Chelsea supporters attended this match?

Four adult tickets were sold for every child's ticket.

b How many children were at the match?

c How many more adults were at the match than children?

During the match, one out of every three children had an ice cream, and 50% of the adults bought three soft drinks.

d Calculate how many ice creams were sold.

e Calculate how many soft drinks were sold.

f Express your answers to parts **d** and **e** as ratios of ice creams : soft drinks in as simple a form as possible.

Prices for laying lawns are directly proportional to the area of the lawn.

For a lawn measuring 8 m × 10 m, there is a charge of £320.

For a lawn measuring 12 m × 12 m, there is a charge of £576.

a How much will it cost to lay a lawn measuring 12 m × 8 m?

b A lawn costs £560. If all lawns are measured to the whole metre, what possible sizes might this lawn be?

The letters in the word MATHEMATICS are written on separate pieces of card and placed in a bag.

a What is the probability that a card chosen randomly will be a T?

b If this first card is not replaced, what is the probability that the first and second cards will both be a T?

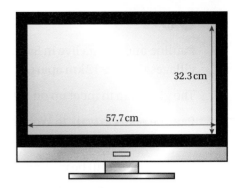

Jenny is shopping for a new television. Having looked at a few she discovers that the size advertised is actually the diagonal length of the screen. Intrigued, she measures her existing TV to see what size it is. Jenny's measurements are shown on the diagram on the right.

Jenny then attempts to measure the diagonal length of her TV. She only has a short ruler but tries to line it up as carefully as she can. She thinks the length is 80 cm.

Explain how you know that Jenny must have measured the diagonal length incorrectly.

Calculate the correct size of Jenny's TV, in inches.

Karen has started making beetroot crisps to sell at the weekly farmers' market. She does not want to buy expensive packing equipment, so she asks her husband and son to pack the crisps for her each week. They must make each packet a similar weight.

At certain times Karen does a random test on some of the packets.

These are the results of one random test:

Husband: 57.8 g, 61.1 g, 62.3 g, 58.9 g, 59.5 g, 60.6 g, 60.1 g, 58.8 g, 58.5 g, 61.3 g, 59.5 g

Son: 58.1 g, 58.7 g, 59.3 g, 58.9 g, 59.3 g, 58.8 g, 60.4 g, 59.1 g, 59.4 g, 58.9 g, 60.2 g

a Display this data in a back-to-back stem and leaf diagram.

b What is the median weight for the crisps packed by:

   i Karen's husband

   ii Karen's son?

The packets have a label that gives the weight of the product as 60 g. Instead of repacking each packet, Karen decided to put a new sticker on the packets giving a new estimated weight.

c What should this new estimated weight be? Give your reasons.

Pauline and Emma live in Salford and Woburn Sands respectively, two villages that are 12 km apart.

The girls plan to meet up on Saturday at Emma's house.

Pauline plans to walk to Woburn Sands, leaving home at 9.10. She can walk at a steady speed of 6 km/h.

Emma's mum will be cycling to Salford and should pass Pauline.

Emma's mum plans to leave Woburn Sands at 9.40. For the first 8 km, she will be travelling at 24 km/h, but the remainder of the route is very steep and she thinks she will not arrive in Salford until 10.40.

Tip

A graph is likely to be helpful here.

a When will Pauline meet Emma's mum?

b How far will Pauline be from home when they meet?

c How far will Emma's mum have travelled?

d What time is Pauline expecting to arrive at Emma's house?

e What is the speed Emma's mum was travelling up the steep hill? Give your answer to one decimal place.

f What distance apart are Pauline and Emma's mum at 10.20?

The graph shows the journey of a car and a moped.

The moped rider travelled from Edinburgh to Glasgow.

The car driver took the same route to Glasgow but returned to Edinburgh.

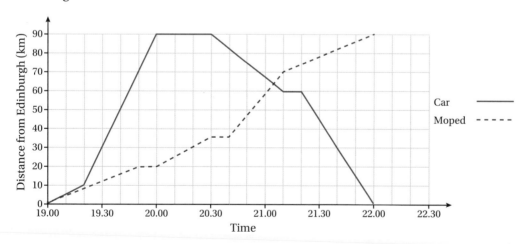

a How far did the moped rider travel in the first 25 minutes?

b How long did it take the car to travel the first 10 km? Can you explain the speed for this first stage of the journey?

c How many stops did the moped rider make and what was the total time she spent resting?

d What was the fastest stage of the journey for the car driver?

e What was the driver's speed at this fast stage?

f At roughly what time did the car and the moped pass each other?

g Roughly how far did the moped rider still have to go at this point?

h What was the average speed for the whole journey for the moped?

i What was the average speed for the return journey for the car?

  21

All standard television screens are mathematically similar. The size of a TV screen size is advertised as the diagonal length, in inches.

Carlos owns a 36.7-inch wide-screen TV. He measures its width as 32.2 inches.

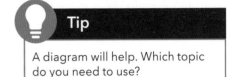
Tip
A diagram will help. Which topic do you need to use?

a What is the aspect ratio (ratio of width to height) for a wide-screen TV?

Eddie is buying a 42-inch wide-screen TV (where 42 inches is the length of the diagonal).

b Work out the length and width of his new TV.

 22

The price of a second-hand car depends on the mileage.

The prices are calculated using the fact that values are inversely proportional to the mileage.

For a car with a mileage of 10 000, the price will be £2000.

a Find the formula used to price these cars.

b What will be the price of a car that has done 20 000 miles?

c A red car is priced at £4000. How many miles has it done?

Sometimes you can use common sense to tell roughly what an answer ought to be. You will probably still need to carry out the calculations, but this can be a useful guide as to whether an answer is correct or not.

Here is an advert.

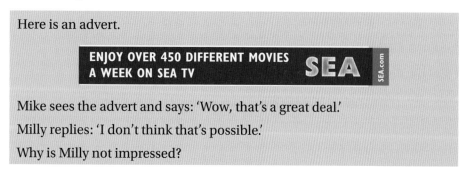

ENJOY OVER 450 DIFFERENT MOVIES A WEEK ON SEA TV   SEA   SEA.com

Mike sees the advert and says: 'Wow, that's a great deal.'

Milly replies: 'I don't think that's possible.'

Why is Milly not impressed?

If you estimate that a movie lasts about 2 hours then you can watch 12 movies in 24 consecutive hours. In a week you could watch $12 \times 7 = 84$. You wouldn't get any sleep, though, so you probably wouldn't enjoy them all! We don't need to do any other calculations to see why Milly is unimpressed.

In A Level Biology there are several formulae used to calculate the actual size (in microns μm: $1\,\mu m = 1 \times 10^{-6}\,m$) of something that has been viewed through a microscope.

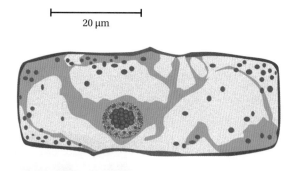

20 μm

The diagram above shows a cell. The students have worked out the actual width of the cell using the formulae, but some of them have got the wrong answer. However, you can tell which of these answers is correct, even if you aren't studying Biology.

a 5.6 μm   **b** 56 μm   **c** 560 μm   **d** 5600 μm

The line above the diagram is 20 μm long and the cell is about three times as wide as that line, so it must be about 60 μm. The answer must therefore be **b** = 56 μm.

The following problems may be solved using more than one method; however, the worked solutions provided at the back of this book are based on the method introduced above.

1 What is wrong with this poster?

> MAY BANK HOLIDAY
> SATURDAY/SUNDAY/MONDAY
> DEALS FROM
>
> GARY'S GROCERS!
>
> *Because this weekend is
> a third longer*

2

$54.7 \times 18.67 \div 11.9$

Which of the answers below is the best estimate for this calculation?

A 50 **B** 100 **C** 73 **D** 75

> **Tip**
>
> Remember that you must explain your answer!

3

Kristie and Amar are both training for the Brighton marathon.

Kristie runs 10 miles each day. Amar runs 15 km each day.

The formula for converting miles to kilometres is: 'Multiply the number of miles by 8, then divide the answer by 5.'

Who do you think will be better prepared for the marathon? Explain your answer.

4

Nathan has just bought a new house. This is a plan of his new garden.

Nathan wants to buy turf (grass) to cover all of the garden apart from the patio, which is made of square paving slabs 80 cm in length. Turf is sold for £2.34 per square metre.

How much will it cost Nathan to buy enough turf?

> **Tip**
>
> Use the paving slabs to work out how wide the garden is.

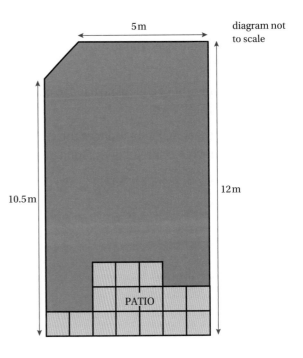

5 m
diagram not to scale
10.5 m
12 m
PATIO

A farmer told Rebecca that she could keep two cows per acre of pasture. This is a plan of her field.

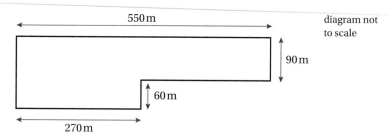

550 m

diagram not to scale

90 m

60 m

270 m

Rebecca knows that an acre is an area of about half a football pitch. She knows that the Old Trafford pitch is 68 m by 105 m.

Approximately how many cows could Rebecca keep on this land?

The ingredients for Fiona's chocolate cake recipe for eight people are shown below.

Cake	Icing
6 eggs	100 g hazelnuts
125 g unsalted butter	125 ml double cream
400 g chocolate spread	120 g dark chocolate
100 g ground hazelnuts	
150 g dark chocolate	

Fiona is having a dinner party and has invited 19 guests. She wants to have enough cake for everyone, including herself, to have one slice each.

a How much dark chocolate should Fiona buy?

b The dark chocolate is available in 200 g bars. How many bars will she need?

c Express the amount of chocolate used to chocolate left over as a ratio in its simplest form.

d On another occasion, Fiona reduces the recipe to serve six people. How much chocolate spread does Fiona need?

In London Zoo there are large number of finches in one big aviary.

The maximum capacity of the aviary is 350 birds so the keeper needs to find out how many birds there are.

He caught 45, put a ring around the leg of each one he caught and released them back into the aviary. A week later he caught 50 finches and found 6 with rings already on.

Does the keeper need to find new homes for any of the finches? If so, how many?

Tip

What fraction of the birds have got a ring? How can you work out how many birds there are altogether?

Sabina is going to carry out a survey on the benefits of exercise for her Physical Education assignment. She has created a questionnaire and is trying to decide who to ask to fill it in:

- the students in her tutor group
- the members of her rugby team
- residents of her grandmother's retirement home.

a For each idea explain why there might be a problem.

The diagram below is an extract from Sabina's questionnaire.

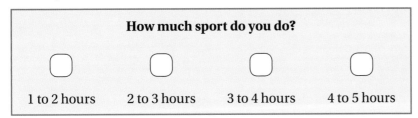

How much sport do you do?

1 to 2 hours   2 to 3 hours   3 to 4 hours   4 to 5 hours

b Write a criticism of the question.

c Write a criticism of the response section.

Vanessa said that the expression for the area of the rectangle shown below is $x^2 - 7x + 6$.

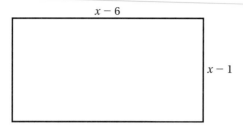

$x - 6$

$x - 1$

Doug said she was wrong. Doug told Vanessa the expression for the area is $2(2x - 7)$.

a Who is correct? Justify your answer.

b What is the expression for the perimeter?

 Put the following numbers in order of size from smallest to largest.

$\sqrt{81}$ $4^2 - 2^3$ $\sqrt[3]{1000}$ $5\sqrt{25} \div 9^0$ $3^{-2} \times 3^2$ $(\sqrt{36})^2$

A plane cruises at a constant speed of 655 miles per hour.

One way to convert miles to kilometres is to divide by 5, then multiply by 8.

a What is the cruising speed of this plane, in km/h?

b At this speed, how long would it take the plane to fly 1746 km?

The distance from Cape Town to London is roughly 9700 km. Tammy made the journey from Cape Town to London on this fast plane cruising at its normal speed.

c What was the shortest time this journey should have taken Tammy?

d Explain why this time is not possible in reality.

Running tracks come in two standard lengths. Indoor tracks are 200 m long and outdoor tracks are 400 m long.

a Simon's event is the 1500 m. How many laps of each track will Simon run in his race?

b Denise will be running both the 5 km and 10 km races. How many laps of each track will she run in each race?

The rule for calculating how long to cook a piece of lamb so that it is medium rare is: '40 minutes per kg and an additional 25 minutes, at 180°C.'

a Create a formula to calculate the cooking time for a piece of lamb of any size.

Uncle Bertie wants to serve Sunday lunch at 12.30. His piece of lamb weighs 3.75 kg and, once taken from the oven, it must stand for 10 minutes before serving.

b Uncle Bertie thinks he needs to put the lamb in the oven at 9 am. Is he right?

Hattie does some form of exercise every day.

Each day she randomly decides to do one of the following: swim 40 lengths, jog 10 km or complete a two-hour cycle ride.

a Draw a sample space diagram showing all the possibilities of the exercise Hattie could do on **two** consecutive days.

b What is the probability that she swims on both days?

c What is the probability that she does not do the same exercise on both days?

A few students from Year 9 and all of Year 8 are at an outdoor activity centre.

They can opt to go swimming, rockclimbing or canoeing. The graphs show how they opted.

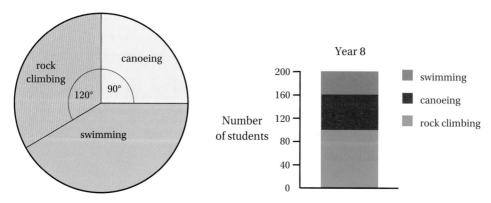

The teacher in charge said that there would be more Year 9 students than Year 8 students in the swimming pools.

Discuss whether this is a correct statement, giving reasons.

Indira asks the boys and girls in her class which pets they own and then makes two pie charts.

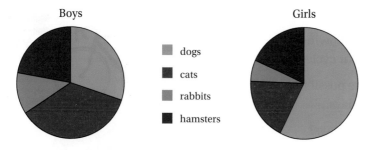

She now wants to use the pie charts to answer questions such as:

- Do more boys or girls own a dog?

- Are rabbits more likely to be owned by boys or girls?

Why can't she answer these sorts of questions from her pie charts?

Two basketball coaches want to do a study of their teams and need the average height of all team members, including the reserves.

Coach McKay uses the data in the table on the right to find the mean height for his team.

Coach Cooksey uses the data from the last health check on each member of his team to find the mean height. The data are as follows:

150 cm, 156 cm, 187 cm, 199 cm, 203 cm, 178 cm, 194 cm, 188 cm, 167 cm, 194 cm, 152 cm, 226 cm, 225 cm, 199 cm, 188 cm, 221 cm, 178 cm, 143 cm, 142 cm, 170 cm.

Team McKay	
Height (cm)	Frequency
$145 \leqslant h < 155$	1
$155 \leqslant h < 165$	2
$165 \leqslant h < 175$	2
$175 \leqslant h < 185$	8
$185 \leqslant h < 195$	3
$195 \leqslant h < 225$	4

a Which coach will have the more accurate mean height for his team? Explain your answer.

b What is the mean height for the McKay team?

c Compare the mean heights of the two teams. Make sure you use the data to justify your comparison.

A glass of orange squash is $\frac{1}{4}$ squash and the rest water. A second, identical glass also contains orange squash; this one is $\frac{5}{6}$ water.

The two glasses are poured into a large drinks bottle.

a What is the fraction of squash in the resulting drink?

Amit is serving drinks at a party. He has two large jugs of fruit punch. The jugs are identical in size, but one contains punch that is $\frac{2}{5}$ apple juice and the other contains punch that is $\frac{3}{10}$ apple juice.

Amit wonders how the drink will change if he pours some from both jugs into a glass.

b Is it possible for Amit to create a drink that is exactly $\frac{1}{2}$ apple juice?

Tip

The strength of the squash in the answer should be between the two strengths in the question.

A health campaign is targeting the high levels of sugar in low fat foods.

One brand of low fat yoghurt is sold in 104 g pots and contains 5.9 g of sugar.

Another yoghurt, not marketed as 'low fat', is sold in 90 g pots and contains 5% sugar.

a Which yoghurt contains more sugar?

b If the guideline daily amount of sugar for an adult is approximately 90 g, how do the two yoghurts compare?

In astronomy, distances are commonly measured in Astronomical Units (AU). 1 AU is the average distance from the Sun to the Earth. 1 AU = 9.3×10^7 miles.

Planet	Distance from Sun in AU
Mercury	0.387
Venus	0.723
Earth	1.000
Mars	1.524
Jupiter	5.203
Saturn	9.523
Uranus	19.208
Neptune	30.087

a Which pair of planets has the shortest possible distance between them?

b What is that distance in miles?

Peter is 2.03 m tall. He and his three shorter friends are planning on going camping. They will be using a traditional tent in the shape of a triangular prism.

What dimensions must their tent be if Peter is to be able to stand upright comfortably and lie flat to sleep alongside his three friends?

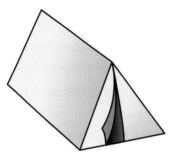

 Tip

You will need to make some assumptions in order to answer this question. You know how tall Peter is, but how much space will he need from side to side?

Sometimes it's useful to make a change to a diagram or situation so that it is easier to see what's going on.

Here is an example.

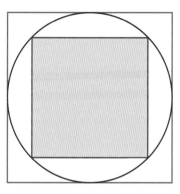

The diagram above shows a red square with a purple circle drawn through its vertices and a blue square drawn so it touches the purple circle on all sides.

What is the relationship between the area of the red square and the area of the blue square? Explain how you know.

Before you turn the page, try to work out the answer.

What ideas have you got?

Here are some things you can try:

- Get a rough idea of what the answer will be. You know that the blue square is bigger than the red square, but it is certainly less than, say, four times the area. This is not the way to work out the final answer, not least because you can't provide an explanation, but it will help you decide if your answer seems reasonable later.
- You don't know any measurements, so do you need to provide some?
- Will it help to call the side length of the red square x? The radius of the circle could be r. It might be useful or it might not.
- Try putting on some extra lines. Will they help?

 Tip

Don't worry if you can't do it straightaway. This is a mathematical problem that is supposed to be difficult. Remember, if you could just 'see' the answer then it wouldn't be a mathematical 'problem'.

Did you manage to solve the problem?

One possible approach is to look at the diagram in a different way.

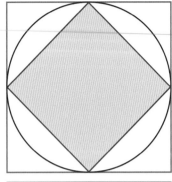

If you rotate the red square nothing vital changes.

The area of the red square is still the same and the purple and blue shapes are unaffected.

Does this help you to see the relationship between the red square and the blue square?

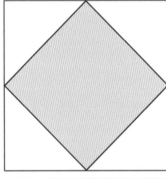

To make this very clear you can remove the circle.

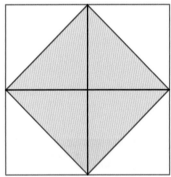

Then you can divide the shape up like this. Now you can explain that the area of the red square is half the area of the blue square.

Tip

The extra lines are helpful after you've rotated the red square.

Here is an example of a full answer.

If you rotate the red square so the vertices of the red square meet the middle of the sides of the blue square you do not change its area.

The two extra lines I have added join the vertices of the red square, cutting it into quarters that are right-angled triangles. These lines also join the middle of the sides of the blue square, cutting it into quarters that are squares.

The total area of the red right-angled triangles is half the area of the blue square.

So the area of the red square is half the area of the blue square.

Tip

You had a rough idea that the area of the blue square was between one and four times the area of the red square, and it is. Estimating the answer can be a useful check that your final answer is sensible.

Tip

You might have answered this question by working out some measurements in terms of x or r instead. This is also a good way to solve the problem.

The following problems may be solved using more than one method; however, the worked solutions provided at the back of this book are based on the method introduced above.

Ben and John are both in the school cricket team. In the last match Ben made 17 runs.

John, who likes puzzles, came up with this formula for the number of runs he made in the same match: 'To work out John's number of runs, multiply Ben's number of runs by 3, then subtract 14.'

Tip

Try a big number and then a small number. What is going on?

a How many runs did John make in that particular match?

b If this formula worked for every match, whom would you consider the better cricketer? Explain why.

c When would this formula fail to work? Explain why.

A spinner has 12 equal sections. The probability of getting purple is $\frac{1}{3}$, red is $\frac{1}{6}$ and green is $\frac{1}{12}$. All other sections are coloured blue.

How many blue sections are there?

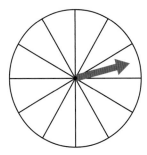

A special eight-sided dice has some of its numbers repeated.

Here is some information about the numbers on the dice:

i All numbers are less than 5.

ii All numbers are positive integers.

iii The probability of rolling a 1 is $\frac{1}{8}$.

iv The probability of rolling a multiple of 2 is $\frac{3}{4}$.

v The probability of rolling a square number is $\frac{3}{8}$.

What is the probability of rolling a prime number?

a What is the probability of throwing a six on an ordinary fair dice?

Bashir told Aaron that if he threw a dice 12 times he should get two sixes.

b Is Bashir correct? Explain your answer.

Tip

Think about your justification and think of alternative arguments.

5

Here is an equilateral triangle.

a How many triangles, similar to the equilateral triangle above, are there in this next diagram?

Tip

There are more than 16.

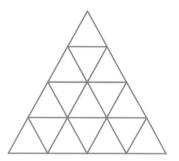

b Justify your answer.

6

The table shows three views of the trapezium prism on the right.

For shapes **A**, **B** and **C** two of the views are given. Draw the top view for each one.

	Front view	Right view	Top view
A			
B			
C			

front

7

Candice has a favourite set of colouring pencils. Some are well-used and have been sharpened many times.

The lengths of her pencils are:

12.5 cm, 11 cm, 11.2 cm, 9 cm, 8.4 cm, 8.7 cm, 6.9 cm, 7.4 cm, 11 cm, 10.7 cm, 11.4 cm and 9.8 cm.

Candice's mother has said that she can have a new set of colouring pencils when the average length of her pencils is less than 10 cm.

If she wants to get new pencils, should Candice tell her mother the modal length, the median length or the mean length?

Jenny is given a set of instructions to create an image.

1 Mark a point on your page and label it 'O'.

2 Draw a 1 cm square with its bottom left-hand corner 1 cm to the right of O.

3 Enlarge this square by a scale factor of 2 about O.

4 Translate the smaller square 1 cm to the left.

5 Rotate the two smaller squares 90° clockwise about the centre of the larger square.

6 Rotate the image (up to and including step 5) 180° about the centre of the larger square.

a What should Jenny's completed image look like?

b How many lines of symmetry does the resulting image have?

c What order of rotational symmetry does the resulting image have?

d Design a set of instructions to create the image below.

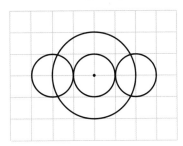

A teacher has asked his class to invent a riddle to describe a polygon of their choice.

This is Jillian's riddle:

I have a prime number of sides.

All my interior angles are obtuse.

I have rotational symmetry of order 5.

What am I?

a Which polygon is Jillian describing? Give as specific an answer as possible.

Gemma hasn't finished her riddle. So far she has the following:

I am a quadrilateral.

I have two pairs of parallel sides.

b Explain which four quadrilaterals Gemma could be referring to.

c Write a final clue for the riddle that can have only one possible correct answer. Then do the same for the other quadrilaterals.

The two plan views below were provided in a test paper.

A   Circle   B   Square

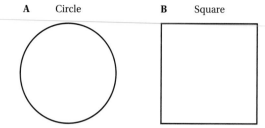

Tip

Don't dismiss any of them without thinking about them from lots of different directions!

Students had to name the 3-D shapes that these plans could represent. Their answers are shown in the table below.

Name	Shape A	Shape B
Matt	cylinder	cube
Jeremy	cone	cuboid
Niall	sphere	cylinder

Who was correct?

Compare each pair of numbers and decide which symbol out of <, > or = should be placed in between them.

a $\dfrac{2}{3}$ 0.66

b 0.25 $\dfrac{8}{32}$

c $\dfrac{3}{11}$ 0.273

d 0.05 $\dfrac{1}{22}$

e 0.5   0.4999... (repeating 9s)

78

Terri is making a birthday cake for her friend. She will write 'Happy Birthday' in icing on the top. She makes a template for the letters, on centimetre-squared paper, as shown below.

a   What is the area of the letter H?

b   What is the area of the letter Y?

c   Does the letter B have a greater area than the letter D?

d   Which letter has the smallest area? How do you know?

Tip

Try to divide the letters up into more familiar shapes. There's more than one way to do this. Try it out and see what works for you.

Sections of decorative fencing are made with metal and wooden rods.

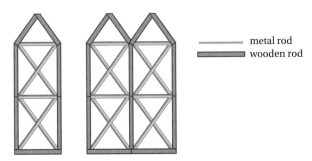

————— metal rod
▨▨▨▨▨ wooden rod

a   How many metal rods will be needed in the next pattern?

b   How many wooden rods are needed for the fourth pattern?

c   Find the number of metal rods needed for the nth pattern (the nth term).

The metal rods cost £2 each and the wooden rods cost £2.50 each.

d   Sue needs a fence made of 12 sections. How much will this cost?

100 people were asked to complete a questionnaire about their pets.

Out of the 100 people, 17 had both a cat and a dog. 54 had either a cat or a dog, but not both. 30 people owned a dog.

a If one person were chosen at random, what is the probability they had neither a cat nor a dog?

b If one person were chosen at random, what is the probability they only owned a cat?

Andy is looking for his homework. This is what he can see on his desk.

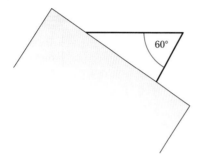

Andy's work is partially covered by a piece of paper.

a Which regular polygon will Andy reveal when he lifts the paper?

Andy wonders how difficult it would be to identify other polygons that have been partially covered.

b Which regular polygon could be hidden under each of these pieces of paper?

i **ii** **iii**

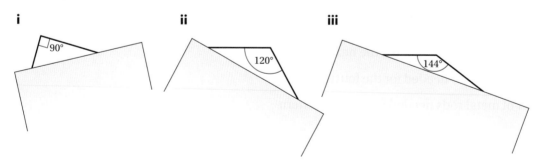

Triangles *ABC* and *XYZ* are similar shapes.

In triangle *ABC*, length *AB* is 8 cm and *AC* is 20 cm.

In triangle *XYZ*, length *XY* is 14 cm and *XZ* is *y* cm.

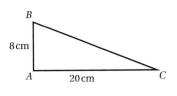 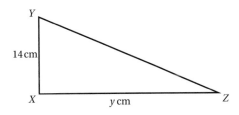

a   What is the length of *XZ*?

b   Work out the area of triangle *ABC* and triangle *XYZ*.

c   Express the area of triangle *ABC* to the area of triangle *XYZ* as a ratio in its simplest form.

d   What type of numbers are in the ratio? Can you explain this?

Arthur has just bought a circular dining table with a diameter of 240 cm. It comes flat-packed to make it easier to transport. Arthur's front door is rectangular and is 2.1 m tall and 1.05 m wide. Will he be able to fit the tabletop through the door?

 Tip

It should be clear that the circular table is not going to fit through the door if held vertically or horizontally. Arthur will need to tilt it to try to get it inside.

Simon is a landscape gardener and he needs to hire a small digger for his next job.

The cost of hiring a digger from JCEs is shown as a straight-line graph.

MoveIt Builders also hire out diggers, but they have a basic fixed charge in addition to their daily charge. Their charges are also shown as a straight-line graph.

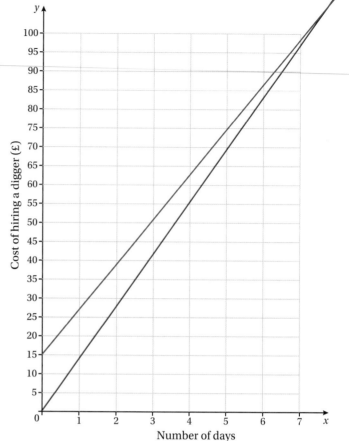

a Which line refers to the charges for each of the companies?

b What is the basic fixed charge made by MoveIt?

c How much per day does JCEs charge?

d Is MoveIt Builders' daily charge more or less than what JCEs charge? By how much?

e What would be the charge if Simon hired the digger from MoveIt Builders for five days?

f What would be the charge if Simon needed the digger for two weeks and he hired it from MoveIt Builders?

g If Simon needed the digger for two weeks, would it be cheaper from MoveIt Builders or JCEs?

h For the two-week period, how much less would it cost to hire from the cheaper company?

Two rectangles are shown below. They are not drawn to scale.

Tip

Try to simplify the side lengths of the rectangles. If you can write them as ordinary numbers the problem will be much simpler.

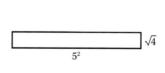

A

$3\sqrt[4]{81}$

$(2^2)^2$

B

5^2

$\sqrt{4}$

a Which rectangle has the greater perimeter?

b Which has the greater area?

20 ✪✪✪

Anna is planning to do something silly to raise money for charity.

She wants to take a bath in cola and needs to know how many bottles of it she will needs to buy.

Anna starts by converting the volume of the bath tub from m³ into cm³. She says: 'There are 100 cm in 1 m so I just need to multiply by 100. $0.15\,\text{m}^3 = 15\,\text{cm}^3$.'

a Explain why Anna is wrong. Her bath tub does **not** have a volume of $15\,\text{cm}^3$.

b Calculate the actual volume of the bath tub in cm³.

c Calculate the number of litres of cola Anna will need to buy.

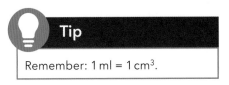

Tip

Remember: $1\,\text{ml} = 1\,\text{cm}^3$.

21 ✪✪✪

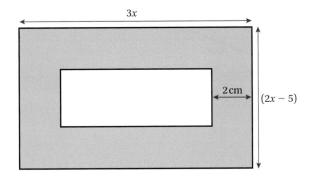

a Create a formula, in terms of x, to calculate the area of the shaded border.

b The area of the border is $204\,\text{cm}^2$. What are the dimensions of the outer rectangle?

Tip

You cut the border into sections and work out the area of each section using algebra.

22 ✪✪✪

Jim went to the local fruit market and bought four apples and five bananas for £2.05.

Peter went to the same fruit market and bought three apples and seven bananas for £2.35.

Jim and Peter asked their maths teacher for an easy method to find the price of an apple and the price of a banana. She told them they could create an equation for the cost of the fruit each of them bought and solve them simultaneously.

a Write the two equations.

b What is the price of one apple?

c What is the price of a banana?

Would you rather:

a receive 80% of £10 or 75% of £12?

b do homework for 20% of 1 hour or $\frac{3}{8}$ of half an hour?

c have 50% of one chocolate cake or 25% of two chocolate cakes (all the cakes are the same size)?

d buy a CD in store for £12.99 or buy it online for the same price but with a 5% discount code and a postage charge of £1.99?

Tip

You could work out the answer to each calculation, but is there an alternative method for some of them?

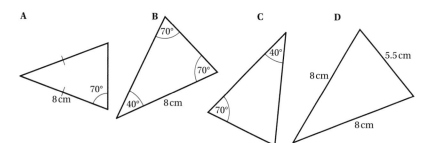

Which of the statements about these triangles are definitely true?

a All four triangles are congruent.

b None of the triangles are congruent.

c Triangles **A**, **B** and **C** are congruent.

d Triangles **B** and **C** are congruent.

e Triangles **A** and **B** are congruent.

Tip

Remember to refer to the conditions for congruence.

In how many ways can you get from flag **A** to flag **B** as shown in the diagram to the right?

a Use a single transformation.

b Use exactly two transformations.

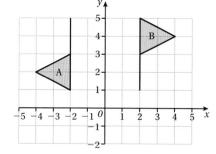

Tip

Remember to provide all the information necessary to describe each transformation fully.

Some questions have more than one answer and you need to provide all the possible answers when solving the problem, without repeating any.

The flag of South Korea is shown on the right.

Around the edge of the central circle there are four 'trigrams'. These are made up of three lines. The one on the top left of the flag has three solid lines.

The one on the top right has a broken line at the bottom and the top, with a solid line in the middle.

If you just use solid lines and broken lines, what fraction of all the possible trigrams (made using three lines) appear on the South Korean flag?

First of all, do you understand the problem? There are other trigrams that could be drawn, such as the one on the right.

It looks as if you will need to work out how many possibilities there are. If you just start writing them down (which is a reasonable starting point) there is a risk that you will miss or repeat some.

These are the ones you have got so far:

A better way to do this would be to work systematically. You could start with three solid lines and no broken lines. That is easy because there is only one possible trigram.

Next you could have two solid lines and one broken line:

This example is systematic in the way the broken line has moved downwards. Can you finish off the rest of the trigrams?

The final list that you get is as follows:

There are eight of them and you can be confident that because you have worked systematically you haven't missed any out, or got any of them twice.

Go back to the original question: **What fraction of all the possible trigrams (made using three lines) appear on the South Korean flag?**

There are four of them on the flag and you know there are eight altogether, so $\frac{1}{2}$ of the trigrams appear on the flag. If you want to test your ability to work systematically try to find all the different diagrams that can be made using four lines.

Here is another problem that can be solved by working systematically.

Without using a calculator decide if 40 735 982 is a square number or not.

Finding the square root of a large number without using a calculator or computer is difficult.

You could start by making a list of square numbers.

That's interesting: The final digit is the same in each row (e.g. 7^2 and 17^2 both end in 9).

Can you explain why that must always happen?

The number in question is 40 735 98**2**. You are looking for a number that ends in a 2. But there aren't any (all square numbers end in either 0, 1, 4, 5, 6 or 9), so 40 735 982 isn't a square number.

(If it ended in a 5 you would need to do some more tests to find out whether it was square.)

n	Square number (n^2)	n	Square number (n^2)
1	1	11	121
2	4	12	144
3	9	13	169
4	16	14	196
5	25	15	225
6	36	16	256
7	49	17	289
8	64	18	324
9	81	19	361
10	100	20	400

The following problems may be solved using more than one method; however, the worked solutions provided at the back of this book are based on the method introduced above.

The first two questions on a worksheet are shown in the diagram below.

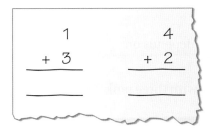

a Using positive integers less than 10, how many different addition questions could be on the rest of the worksheet? (Note the order in addition is not important, so 4 + 2 is the same as 2 + 4, and therefore these do not count as different questions.)

b If another worksheet only includes negative integers greater than −10, how many **different answers** to addition calculations could there be?

You are only allowed to add the numbers 3 and 5. For example you can make 13 by doing 3 + 5 + 5. You can use each number more than once or not at all (for example 3 + 3).

What is the largest number you cannot make in this way?

Which number under 18 has the most factors?

The tiles on Sajan's kitchen floor are regular hexagons with a side length of 130 mm.

a Calculate the perimeter of the shaded section of tiles in the diagram below. Give your answer in centimetres.

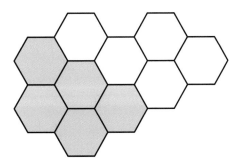

b A different section of tiles has a perimeter of 156 cm. How many tiles are there in this section?

Charmaine makes bracelets. These include flowers made with pink beads and blue beads. Each flower consists of one pink bead surrounded by six blue beads.

The number of flowers she puts on a friendship bracelet depends on the size of the bracelet.

a How many blue beads would she need for a bracelet with three pink beads?

b The number of blue beads follows a pattern. What is the *n*th term for this pattern?

Connor rolls a biased dice 50 times and gets 15 sixes.

a How many sixes should he expect if he rolls the dice 100 times?

b After many rolls Connor has recorded 105 sixes; how many times do you think he has thrown the dice?

c How many sixes should he expect if he rolls the dice 1200 times?

At St Mary's School there are 98 Year 7 students, 105 Year 8 students, 110 Year 9 students, 108 Year 10 and 99 Year 11 students. The headteacher must pick one student at random to represent the school in a parade.

What is the probability the headteacher will pick a Year 9 student? Simplify your answer.

 Look at each pair of multiplications below and decide in each case which of the pair gives the **larger** answer.

a 10×7 or 11×6

b -44×5 or 44×-5

c $972\,310 \times 0$ or 1×1

d 91×-2 or 59×3

Which of the following calculations has the smallest answer?

i $100 \div (5^2 \times 2)$ **ii** $620 \times 4 \div 248$

iii $81 - 37 \times 2$ **iv** $-27 \div -3 + 12$

 5 ☐ 2 ☐ 10 ☐ –3

Insert the operators +, – and × into the three boxes above. You should use all of them once each.

In how many ways can you achieve a negative result?

Tip

In how many ways can you arrange the three operators in the spaces provided? Can you find a systematic way of recording all the possible arrangements to be sure that you've considered them all?

Martin helps himself to sandwiches from a buffet lunch. He notices that the sandwiches have all been cut into identical triangles.

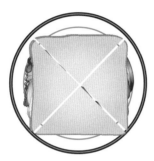

Martin realises that he has placed his sandwiches so that they fit together to create a square. He wonders how many different polygons he can create by arranging two or more sandwiches on his plate.

a Assuming that Martin matches the edges of the sandwiches, how many different polygons can he create, using:

i exactly two sandwiches?

ii exactly three sandwiches?

iii all four sandwiches?

b Is it possible for Martin to create all of the special types of quadrilateral using two or more sandwiches from his plate?

Tip

Think of a logical way of trying out all the possible arrangements of the sandwiches.

You also need to decide on a sensible way of recording your findings so that you can check you have found **all** the possible polygons.

Where possible, use the correct mathematical name for each polygon you find.

12

Three students are asked the question: **What is the smallest integer that is exactly divisible by 2 and 3?**

The students give three correct answers to this question:

Gemma says: 'It must be 6 because $2 \times 3 = 6$.'

Lidia says: 'It must be 6 because it can't be 4 (3 doesn't work), it can't be 5 (2 and 3 both don't work), but it can be 6.'

Harry says: 'It must be 6 because the 2 times table goes: 2, 4, 6, 8 … and the 3 times table goes: 3, 6, 9 …. So 6 is the first number that is in both lists.'

If the students are then asked the question: **What is the smallest integer that is exactly divisible by 2, 3 and 4?**

a i What would Gemma's answer be (assuming she used the same method as above)?

ii Is Gemma correct?

iii Would Lidia or Harry be correct if they applied their methods?

iv Can you think of another method to answer this question?

A final question is asked: **What is the smallest integer that is exactly divisible by 3, 5 and 6?**

b Select an approach from the methods given above to help you to solve this problem.

13

A factory makes packing boxes for cylinders.

Each box is a cuboid measuring 40 cm by 40 cm, with a height of 15 cm.

a What are the maximum dimensions (radius and height) of the cylinders that can fit into each box?

b Make a guess as to which box has the most unused space.

c Use calculations to check your guess. What did you find?

Tip

The volume of a cylinder is $\pi \times r^2 \times h$.

In a school's packed lunch, students can have a sandwich and either crisps, fruit or a yoghurt, plus a bottle of water or carton of fruit juice.

a   List all the different possible combinations of packed lunches.

b   Kai randomly picks up a packed lunch. What is the probability that Kai's packed lunch will include a yoghurt?

c   If each combination has the same chance of being prepared how many out of 330 children will have crisps in their packed lunch?

Tania is asked to think randomly of a number greater than 1 but less than 50.

What is the probability that Tania chooses:

a   an even number?

b   an odd number?

c   a multiple of five?

d   27?

e   a factor of 48?

In Ahmed's money box there is a total of £47 and this includes twelve 50p coins and nine £1 coins. The rest of the coins are £2 coins.

Ahmed wants to shake one coin out of his money box.

What is the probability that it will be a £2 coin?

Timi's dad has two sets of jelly moulds. In one set he has a circle, star and triangle mould. In the other set he has a heart, a rabbit and a car.

Timi wants his dad to make some jelly using one mould from each set.

a Show all the different combinations possible.

b Timi's dad randomly picks a mould from each set. What is the probability that he will pick the star and the rabbit?

Julie has eight black pens, one red pen and three blue pens in her pencil case.

Julie needs a pen, so she randomly picks one from her pencil case.

a What is the probability that it is a blue pen?

Julie puts her pen back in her pencil case. In the next lesson, Julie needs a pen again and Tommy wants to borrow one as well. Julie randomly picks a pen for herself and one for Tommy.

b What is the probability Julie picks blue pens for both of them?

Max has 12 panels of fencing that he will join together to make a run for his pet rabbits. Each panel is 60 cm long. He arranges them so that they enclose a square.

a What is the area of the pen that Max has created?

Adam thinks he can make the run larger by rearranging the panels into a rectangle, where the length is double the width.

b Is Adam correct?

Kim thinks she can make the run larger by rearranging the panels into an equilateral triangle.

c Is Kim right?

> **Tip**
>
> Remember, you must always justify your answer. Make sure that you explain your answer so that someone reading it will be convinced.

Four similar triangles are placed together to form the pattern shown below.

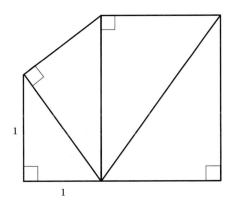

diagram not to scale

1

1

a Show that the area of the largest triangle is four times that of the smallest triangle.

b Do the four triangles meet on a straight line?

Find values for a, b and c that make the following equation true.

$$245 = 1^a + 2^b + 3^c$$

10 If you don't know what to do, do something

If you are having difficulties with a problem, you might encounter a strange situation. You could call it 'the problem with problem solving' as shown on the right.

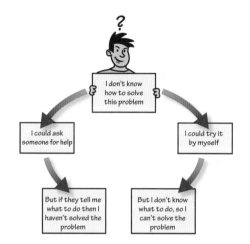

If you find yourself in this situation one strategy is: 'If you don't know what to do, do something.' But make sure the 'something' you do is useful.

Some things that are **not** useful include colouring a picture (unless it is a problem about colouring), or writing the question out in perfect handwriting. These are just things that keep you busy, but are unlikely to help.

The previous chapters in this book outlined different problem-solving strategies. If you are stuck, try one of these strategies. If the first strategy you try doesn't work, try a different one.

You might find it helpful to write down the things you do know (for example the key ideas from the question) and which areas of mathematics these relate to.

Here is an example.

> Ben bought a bag of rice at the supermarket. He wonders how many grains of rice are in the bag. Can you help him?

All sorts of things seem to make this question impossible to answer.

Not every bag of rice has exactly the same number of grains of rice in it.

Different varieties of rice are different sizes (for example, long grain rice is longer than risotto rice).

Individual grains vary in size.

We don't know how big the bag is. If he has bought a 1 kg bag then there will be approximately twice as many grains as in a 500 g bag.

You will have realised by now that there isn't going to be an exact answer, so you need to work out a rough answer. It is often useful to work out a ball-park figure, and as long as it is of the right order of magnitude (which means it has roughly the correct number of digits) then that will be reasonable.

If you decide a problem is difficult and do nothing then it won't get solved! You could start by trying some things that might be useful.

Count every grain of rice in a bag.

Nice idea, but you haven't got a bag of rice and the answer is probably rather big, so it will take a long time. Besides, that's counting rather than doing maths, so let's try something else.

Weigh a single grain and then work out how many grains there will be in 1 kg.

This is nicer, no counting involved! A 2p coin weighs 7 g, so a single grain of rice will be extremely light, and certainly less than 1 g. Your scales aren't accurate enough to do this (and you don't have any rice to weigh anyway).

Find out how many grains weigh 1 g and then multiply by 1000.

This is useful because it uses the fact that 1000 g = 1 kg.

Find out how big a grain of rice is.

Can you draw a picture of an uncooked grain of rice? (Uncooked rice is smaller than the fluffy, cooked rice.) The rice in the drawing on the right is about $\frac{1}{2}$ cm long and maybe 2 mm high.

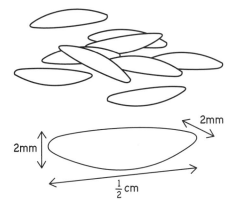

What shape is a grain of rice?

It's a bit like a cylinder but with sloping ends. In fact, it is roughly a cuboid! You could work out the rough volume of the grain of rice by assuming it is a cuboid that is $\frac{1}{2}$ cm by 2 mm by 2 mm.

Work out the volume of a bag of rice and compare this with the volume of a grain of rice. In the kitchen cupboard at home you are probably used to seeing 1 kg bags of food (sugar, flour, pasta, rice, etc). You can get a mental image of a 1 kg bag of sugar. Using your ruler to help, visualise the size. This should be about 10 cm by 15 cm by 8 cm.

But the units are all different. That is awkward, so you should work in mm.

The volume of a single grain of rice is about 5 mm × 2 mm × 2 mm. This is 20 mm³.

The volume of the bag is about 100 mm × 150 mm × 80 mm. This is 1 200 000 mm³.

1 200 000 ÷ 20 = 60 000, so there are roughly 60 000 grains in a bag.

Ask yourself whether this seems reasonable.

If 60 000 grains of rice weigh 1 kg then about 60 of them would weigh 1 g. So this does seem possible. The errors in your estimate of the sizes are likely to be outweighed by the fact that rice grains are not cuboids, but they also don't fit together perfectly in the bag.

To start with you had no idea what to do. You tried out some different ideas and eventually worked out an answer.

The following problems may be solved using more than one method; however, the worked solutions provided at the back of this book are based on the method introduced above.

Dance United are touring North America. They are a group of 15 dancers and need to pay as little as possible for hotel rooms. In North America there is a chain of motels that uses the following formula for its room charges: '$75 for one person, plus $35 per extra person.' In Dallas, the motel only has rooms with three beds. In Las Vegas the motel has rooms with four beds. In San Francisco, there are only two rooms left that have six beds, the rest of the rooms have two beds.

a How much did the accommodation cost in Dallas?

b How much cheaper was it to stay in Las Vegas, compared with Dallas?

c Which was the cheapest city for the dancers to stay in?

Sarah knows her height is 5 ft 10 inches. Leon's height is 180 cm and he tells Sarah he is taller than she is.

Given that 1 inch is approximately the same as 2.5 cm, is Leon correct?

Tarjhay is given £40 for his birthday and he really wants to buy his favourite basketball team's kit. The kit costs $65. The exchange rate is £1 = $1.70.

How much money will he have left?

Jenny watched a fitness group running laps of the playing field shown in the diagram below. Most people completed three laps before stopping.

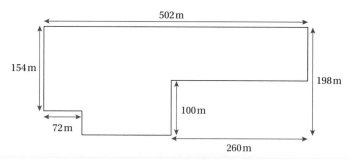

a How far did most people run? Give your answer in kilometres.

Two of the runners continued for another four laps.

b How far did those two people run? Give your answer in kilometres.

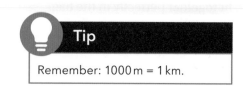

Tip

Remember: 1000 m = 1 km.

Jyoti and Laura are making towers with cubes.

Between them they have 12 cubes, each of different sizes.

There is a 1 cm cube, a 2 cm cube, a 3 cm cube, a 4 cm cube and so on, up to the biggest cube, which measures 12 cm along each edge.

For the first towers they make, Jyoti uses the six smallest cubes and Laura uses the six largest.

a How much taller is Laura's tower compared with Jyoti's?

The girls then decide to make towers of the same height using all of the cubes.

b Work out a combination of cubes that each girl could have.

 Which of the statements about the number 12 345 678 912 are true?

i It is a multiple of 3.

ii It is a prime number.

iii Dividing the number by 5 leaves a remainder of 2.

iv It is a multiple of 4.

Tip

How can you quickly decide if a number is a multiple of 3? Or 4?

Grandad Jones is twice as old as his son Geoff. Geoff is 28 years older than his son Paul.

The total age of the three family members is 112 years.

What ages are Grandad Jones, Geoff and Paul?

The formula for calculating the cost of placing an advert in a local newspaper is $c = 17n + 60$, where n is the number of words and c is the cost, in pence.

a Find the cost of an advert that contains 55 words.

b Sally placed an advert and it cost £21. How many words did Sally's advert have?

Jolene wants to place an advert to sell her bicycle. She only wants to spend a maximum of £10 on her advert.

c What is the maximum number of words Jolene can use to keep the cost to £10 or less?

Mo is running a marathon this weekend. He will carry a water bottle as shown in the diagram below. He has bought some energy powder that dissolves in water.

15 cm

8 cm

To the nearest half-scoop, how many scoops of the energy powder should he use to fill the bottle to a depth of 15 cm with energy drink?

For every eight students going on a school trip there must be an accompanying teacher. 140 students want to go on the next school trip.

a How many teachers will need to be on this trip?

Some staff members have decided they want to join the trip. There are now 21 staff members available for the trip.

b How many extra students could go on the trip?

It was too late to take extra students, so the original 140 students went with the extra staff.

c What is the new ratio of students to staff?

For a set of eight whole numbers, the following information is known:

The biggest number is 16.

Mean = 7.5.

Mode = 3 and 5.

Range = 15.

What could the numbers be?

Tip

You will need to start by calculating the volume of the water bottle.

Tip

Remember: 1 cm³ = 1 ml.

Tip

There is more than one answer.

Harvey translated a shape by the vector $\begin{pmatrix} 2 \\ 3 \end{pmatrix}$ and got the following image shown in the diagram below.

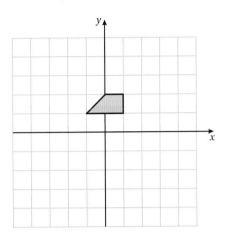

a Where was Harvey's original shape?

Harvey rotated another shape 90° clockwise about the origin and got the image on the right.

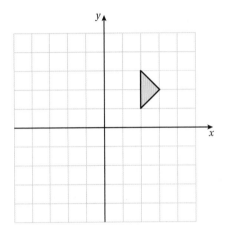

b Where was Harvey's original shape?

Harvey rotated a further shape 90°anti-clockwise about (1, 1), and then translated it by the vector $\begin{pmatrix} -3 \\ 2 \end{pmatrix}$ to achieve the final image shown below.

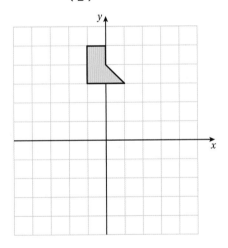

c Where was Harvey's original shape?

> **Tip**
>
> How can you work backwards through this problem? What are the 'inverse' transformations that need to be applied?

13

A magic square has the property that the numbers in each row, column and diagonal add up to the same thing (the 'Magic Number').

For the magic square shown below, the Magic Number is 2.1.

0.74		
$\frac{129}{150}$		
		$\frac{33}{50}$

Complete the magic square.

14

Flo visits a garden centre. She buys a wooden planter box in the shape of a cuboid that measures 1 m × 80 cm × 70 cm. She also buys compost to fill the planter. Compost is sold in 50-litre bags.

a What is the smallest number of bags of compost Flo needs to buy to fill the planter completely?

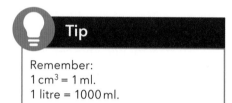

Tip

Remember:
$1 \text{ cm}^3 = 1 \text{ ml}$.
1 litre = 1000 ml.

The bags of compost cost £5.99 each and are part of a special offer: 3 for £12.

b How much will it cost Flo to buy the compost?

c How much money does Flo save by taking advantage of the special offer?

15

A field is 80 m long by 70 m wide. A goat is tethered to a pole in the centre of the field using a rope 15 m long.

A farmer plants wheat across the width of the field for 30 m from one end. The goat eats all the wheat it can access.

Draw a scale drawing and shade the area of wheat the goat eats.

16

Alesha has a pack of playing cards. She tells Jamie she could pick two aces from the pack without looking at them. Alesha picks her first card; she keeps this and then picks her second card.

a What is the probability of Alesha picking two aces if she chooses at random? Simplify your answer as much as possible.

b What is the probability of Alesha picking two red kings instead?

17

Female rabbits can have four to eight kits (baby rabbits) per litter.

The probability of the number of kits a pregnant female rabbit will have per litter is given in the table below.

Number of kits per litter	4	5	6	7	8
Probability	0.1	0.2	0.3	0.3	x

a What is the probability that a randomly picked pregnant female rabbit will have eight kits in one litter?

b What is the probability that two randomly picked pregnant female rabbits have a total of 16 kits in one breeding season?

c What is the probability that two randomly picked pregnant female rabbits have a total of ten kits in one breeding season?

18

There are approximately 5×10^9 red blood cells per millilitre of blood. James's blood volume is approximately 9 pints.

If James gives a 10% blood donation, how many red blood cells are left?

One imperial pint equals approximately 568.261 ml. It is acceptable to round this value to 568 ml or even 570 ml for use in calculations.

Two identical triangles are drawn using two diameters and two vertical lines inside a circle with a radius of 7 cm as shown below.

Tip

You have a right-angled triangle, another angle and a side length. What topic can you use?

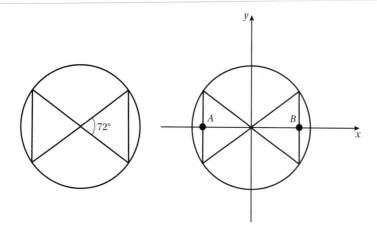

If this diagram is placed on a coordinate grid so that the centre of the circle is located at the origin, what will be the coordinates of points *A* and *B*?

a

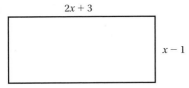

This is $6x + 4$

To work out the perimeter of a rectangle, you need to add up the sides. To work out the area you multiply the two sides.

A diagram will help.

An expression for the perimeter

b The perimeter is 70 cm, so $6x + 4 = 70$.

$x = 11$

The longest side is $2x + 3$, which is 25 cm.

Solve $6x + 4 = 70$ for x.

c The width is $x - 1$, which is 10 cm.

The area is therefore $25 \times 10 = 250 \text{ cm}^2$

To work out the area of a rectangle you multiply the length by the width. This means you need to work out the width.

2 Here is the top cylinder:

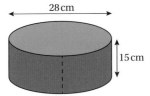

The circumference of the large cylinder $= \pi \times$ diameter.

When this is cut along the dotted line it can be unwrapped to give a rectangle, where the height of the rectangle is the same as the height of the cylinder and the width is the same as the circumference of the cylinder. The diagram helps to show what is going on.

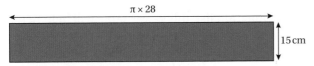

Surface area of the top cylinder is $\pi \times 28 \times 15 = 420\pi$
($= 1319.4689... \text{ cm}^2$)

The area of the curved surface of the large cylinder = height × length (circumference).

The middle one is $\pi \times 22 \times 10 = 220\pi$
($= 691.15038... \text{ cm}^2$)

Calculate the circumference and area of the curved surface of the medium cylinder.

The lowest one is $\pi \times 16 \times 10 = 160\pi$
($= 502.65482... \text{ cm}^2$)

Calculate the circumference and area of the curved surface of the small cylinder.

The total is therefore 800π
($= 2513.3 \text{ cm}^2$ 1 dp)

Round the answer to 1 d.p.

3

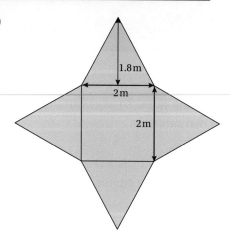

$2\,\text{m} \times 2\,\text{m} = 4\,\text{m}^2$

$\frac{1}{2} \times 2\,\text{m} \times 1.8\,\text{m} = 1.8\,\text{m}^2$

$1.8\,\text{m}^2 \times 4 = 7.2\,\text{m}^2$

$4\,\text{m}^2 + 7.2\,\text{m}^2 = 11.2\,\text{m}^2$

A diagram shows all of the shapes. The triangles are all the same.

Area of square base = length × width.

Area of one triangular face = $\frac{1}{2}$ base × height.

Area of all four triangular faces.

Total surface area of tent (square base + four triangular faces).

4

Lavender

Geranium

Draw a diagram of two of the rows.

There must be 7 rows of geraniums ($70 \div 10 = 7$), so there are 8 rows of lavender because it starts and finishes with a row of lavender.

$6 \times 8 = 48$ lavender plants

5 Of the 54 workers surveyed, 22 preferred coffee, 16 preferred tea and 16 preferred hot chocolate.

Peter was incorrect. Tea is not the most popular drink, coffee is the most popular hot drink among the workers, and hot chocolate is equally as popular as tea.

A diagram like this 2-way table will help here.

	Hot chocolate	Tea	Coffee	Total
Women	8	9	12	29
Men	8	7	10	25
Total	16	16	22	54

6

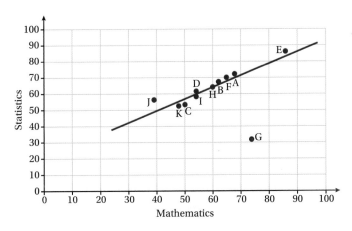

An easy way to see what is going on is to draw a scattergraph.

a The line of best fit suggests that 70 statistics marks would link with about 66 mathematics marks.

b This is a very good positive correlation, so the prediction is likely to be fairly accurate.

c Student G is an outlier.

---

7 **a** $25x + 75$ or $50x - 75$

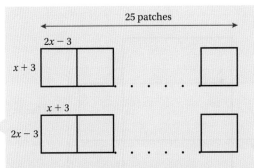

There are 25 patches in each row.

The width could be $25(x + 3) = 25x + 75$

or it could be $25(2x - 3) = 50x - 75$

b $64x - 96$ or $32x + 96$

$32(2x - 3)$ or it could be $32 (x + 3)$

c $64x - 96 = 64 \times 5 - 96 = 224 \, \text{cm}$

$x + 3 = 8$

$25x + 75 = 25 \times 5 + 75 = 200 \, \text{cm}$

$x = 5$

This is 2.24 m by 2 m.

The alternative version gives a size of 1.75 m by 2.56 m.

8 **a** 4 metres

One less than five bricks = 4

b 4 bricks

Length + 1 = number of bricks

c

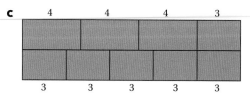

Any combination of 4 and 3 to total 15.

4 m + 4 m + 4 m + 3 m

3 m + 3 m + 3 m + 3 m + 3 m

4 m + 4 m + 4 m + 3 m would need: 5 + 5 + 5 + 4 bricks (for every metre of plank there is one extra brick)

or

3 m + 3 m + 3 m + 3 m + 3 m would need: 4 + 4 + 4 + 4 + 4 bricks

d 19 bricks

20 bricks

9

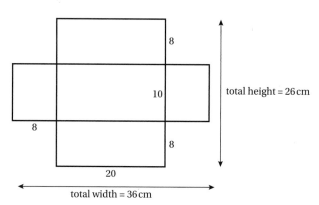

A diagram showing all the faces of the box will help.

total height = 26 cm

total width = 36 cm

a $20 \times 10 + 10 \times 8 \times 2 + 20 \times 8 \times 2 = 680 \, cm^2$

b

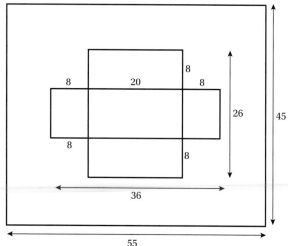

45 – 26 = 19 cm, which is more than enough to go across the rim of the box and inside.

55 – 36 = 19 cm, so it will work in that direction too.

The piece of paper **is** big enough.

10 **a**

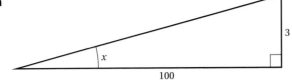

$$\tan x = \frac{3}{100}$$

$x = 1.7°$ (1 d.p.)

b

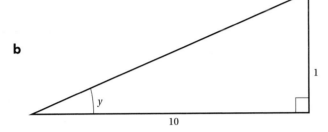

$$\tan y = \frac{1}{10}$$

$y = 5.7°$ (1 d.p.)

The difference between the slopes is 3.9922°. It is 4.0° steeper.

11 The diameter of the cherry tree is 3 m. I will assume it has a radius of 1.5 m. This means the tree can be planted anywhere that is at least 1.5 m away from the edge of the lawn.

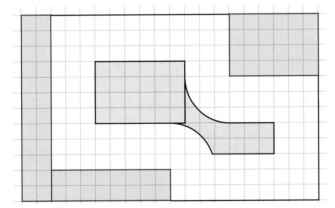

You can choose any scale you like.

To show where the cherry tree can go there are straight lines 1.5 m away from the edge of the lawn and arcs (parts of circles) at the corners of the flower bed and the vegetable patch.

This diagram has a scale of two squares to 1 m. The shaded area is where the cherry tree can be planted.

12 The helicopters cover 25 km from each town, so we need two circles. The fire brigade covers the section closer to B than A, so we need the locus of points equidistant from both towns.

Here the scale is 1 cm = 5 km (you might have chosen a different scale).

Start with a line of 8 cm (to represent the 40 km distance between the towns).

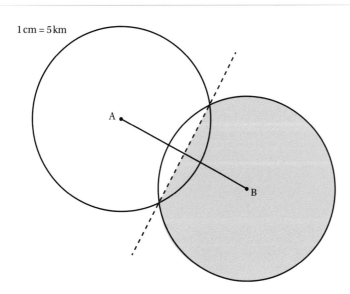

1 cm = 5 km

With compasses draw a circle centre B and radius 5 cm.

With compasses draw a circle centre A and radius 5 cm.

The locus of points equidistant from B and A is the perpendicular bisector of line AB.

Shade the region that is closer to B than A and covered by the helicopter.

13

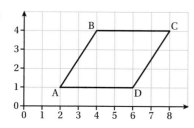

A diagram of the situation helps you see what is going on.

a $\overrightarrow{CD} = \begin{pmatrix} -2 \\ -3 \end{pmatrix}$

b $\overrightarrow{AB} = \begin{pmatrix} 2 \\ 3 \end{pmatrix}$

The length AB is the same as the length CD but the vectors are in opposite directions.

c Hence ABCD is a parallelogram – a four sided shape with two sets of parallel sides.

BC is $\begin{pmatrix} 4 \\ 0 \end{pmatrix}$ and AD is $\begin{pmatrix} 4 \\ 0 \end{pmatrix}$ so BC is parallel to AD

AB is $\begin{pmatrix} 2 \\ 3 \end{pmatrix}$ and DC is $\begin{pmatrix} 2 \\ 3 \end{pmatrix}$ so AB is parallel to DC

14

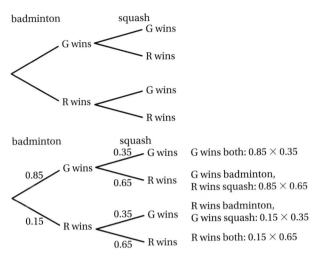

Start with a diagram to show what is going on.

Then fill in the probabilities.

a $0.85 \times 0.35 = 0.2975$

b $0.15 \times 0.35 = 0.0525$

c $0.85 \times 0.65 + 0.15 \times 0.35 = 0.605$

15

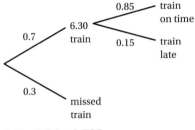

A tree diagram might be useful here.

$0.7 \times 0.85 = 0.595$

16

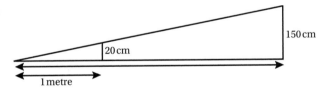

A good diagram shows that this is a question about similar triangles.

The scale factor of the enlargement is $150\,cm \div 20\,cm$ = 7.5.

$1\,m \times 7.5 = 7.5\,m$

The image needs to be 7.5 larger to fill the screen. This means that the projector needs to be 7.5 times further away.

17 **a i, ii**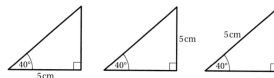

There are three possible triangles that fit Harriet's description.

iii She could say that the hypotenuse is 5 cm.

Other answers are possible too.

For only one triangle to be possible, Harriet must make sure that her conditions follow one of the conditions of congruence:

SSS, SAS, ASA, AAS or RHS

b i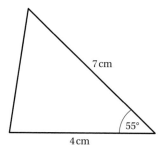

There is only one triangle that satisfies Janet's conditions because she has given SAS.

ii A scale drawing will enable you to measure the length of the third side as 5.7 cm to the nearest mm.

18 **a** scattergraph, histogram, bar chart, pie chart.

b A scattergraph won't be appropriate because you don't have two pieces of information about the same thing.

A histogram only works for numerical data.

A bar chart would work, as would a pie chart.

c

Tea
Americano
Espresso
Latte
Cappuccino

In shop **A**, tea and americanos are much more popular that the other drinks.

In shop **B**, lattes and cappuccinos are much more popular.

	Shop A		Shop B	
Type of drink	Frequency	Angle	Frequency	Angle
Tea	28	28 × 5 = 140	15	15 × 4 = 60
Americano	22	22 × 5 = 110	8	8 × 4 = 32
Espresso	9	9 × 5 = 45	6	6 × 4 = 24
Latte	6	6 × 5 = 30	35	35 × 4 = 140
Cappuccino	7	7 × 5 = 35	26	26 × 4 = 104
Total	72	360°	90	360°

For shop **A**: 360° ÷ 72 = 5°. For shop **B**: 360° ÷ 90 = 4°.

19 **a**

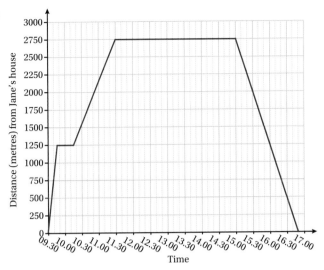

Horizontal lines indicate there is no change in the distance travelled.

b Distance travelled = 1500 m

Time taken = 1.25 h

Speed = $\dfrac{1.5\,\text{km}}{1.25}$ = 1.2 km/h

Speed = $\dfrac{\text{distance}}{\text{time}}$

c Distance = 2750 m

Time = 1 h 40 min = $1 + \dfrac{40}{60}$ hour = $1\frac{2}{3}$ h

Speed = 2.75 km ÷ $1\frac{2}{3}$

= 1.65 km/h

20 **a**

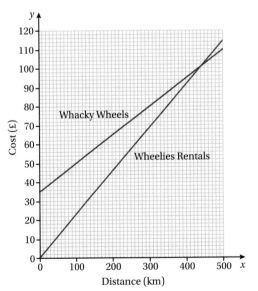

The graph is helpful in answering the rest of this question.

b Wheelies Rentals

Whacky Wheels: £35 + £75 = £110

Wheelies Rentals: 500 × £0.23 = £115

c £5

21 **a**

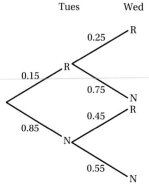

Tues   Wed

Key
R = rain
N = no rain

A tree diagram is often helpful in probability questions

b $0.15 \times 0.25 = 0.0375$

c $(0.15 \times 0.75) + (0.85 \times 0.45) = 0.495$

22 **a**

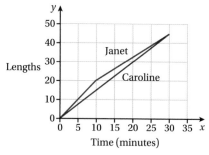

200 students

let studying Chemistry be event C

let studying Physics be event P

let studying Maths be event M

b $\dfrac{17}{200}$

c $\dfrac{68}{200} = \dfrac{17}{50}$

23 **a**

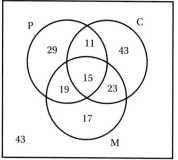

b no

The line for Caroline's graph is always below Janet's so there is no time when Caroline has swum further than Janet.

c 20 min

d $\dfrac{45}{30} = 1.5$ lengths per minute

24 **a**

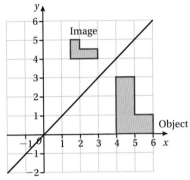

Choose a shape without any symmetry to easily see what is going on.

b

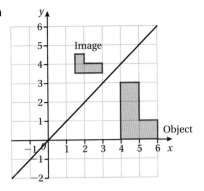

The orientation and size of the final image are the same when the transformations are carried out in a different order, but it ends up in a different place.

1 $\sqrt{64} = 8$

You can't tell immediately, but it seems sensible to evaluate to $\sqrt{64}$.

$10\sqrt{64} = 10 \times 8 = 80$

$10\sqrt{64} = 80$ so the statement $(10\sqrt{64} < 80)$ is false.

2

A sleeper is 8.5 feet long.

$8.5 \times 30 = 255\,\text{cm} = 2.55\,\text{m}$

It is sensible to first convert the length of a sleeper to centimetres and then metres.

An alternative would be to convert the length of the border into feet.

$\dfrac{20\,\text{m}}{2.55\,\text{m}} = 7.8...$ so he needs 8 sleepers

$8 \times £22 = £176$

---

3 $2 \times (6\,\text{m} + 4\,\text{m}) = 20\,\text{m}$

$85\,\text{cm} \div 100 = 0.85\,\text{m}$

You can't work out the cost, but you can work out the perimeter of the living room.

$20 - 2 \times 0.85 = 18.3\,\text{m}$

Subtract the two doors.

It looks as though you need to buy whole metres of skirting board, so 19 m is needed.

$£4.31 \times 19 = £81.89$

---

4 **a** $3 : 5$ gives 8 parts.

Start by working out the number of parts in the ratio.

$32 \div 8 = 4$

$3 \times 4 = 12$ non-calculator questions on each test and 20 calculator questions.

b 15 tests $\times$ 20 = 300 calculator questions

c $15 \times 32 = 480$ questions, so each teacher will write 240 questions.

This is complicated, so let's find out how many questions there are altogether.

Miss Smith will write $15 \times 12 = 180$ non-calculator questions and $240 - 180 = 60$ calculator questions.

60 of those are calculator questions and 180 are non-calculator.

d $\dfrac{60}{180} = \dfrac{1}{3}$

5

Because of the way the paper has been folded you know the marked angle is 45°.

360° ÷ 45° = 8, so 8 of the kites will fit together.

6 12 × 5 = 60

> This is a challenging problem.
>
> If the mean of 5 numbers is 12, what do you know? When you work out the mean of five numbers you add them up and divide by 5, so before the sum was divided by 5 it must have totalled 60 (because 60 ÷ 5 = 12).

60 ÷ 4 = 15

> You also know that there are 15 parts in the ratio.

4 : 4 : 12 : 16 : 24

The largest numbers is 24

> Multiplying the numbers in the ratio by 4 gives these figures, and the largest one is 24.

7 300 000 000 ÷ 10 = 30 000 000 miles in one year

30 000 000 ÷ 365 = 82 191.78 miles in one day

82 191.78 ÷ 24 = 3 424.657 5 miles per hour

> Start by working out what you can.
>
> You need to assume that the probe travels at a constant speed.
>
> The probe travelled 300 000 000 miles in 10 years. Work out how many miles it travelled per hour.

3 424.657 5 ÷ 290 = 11.8

The probe was travelling about 12 times as fast as the car.

> Divide this by 290.

8 Some of the shapes have symmetry:

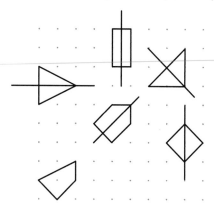

So there is only one that does not have any lines of symmetry.

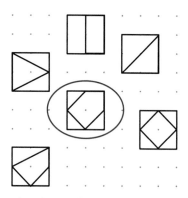

The shape that is circled is the only one that is not half of the square, so this could be the odd one out.

Maybe this is something to do with the perimeters of the shapes.

The perimeters are quite difficult to work out because of the diagonal lines involved, so it doesn't look likely that the perimeters are involved.

Perhaps it is a symmetry problem. Try checking the symmetry of the shapes.

Maybe this is something to do with the areas of the shapes.

To work out the areas, you could draw a 2 by 2 square around them all.

9 **a**

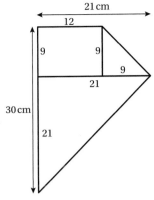

Rectangle: $12 \times 9 = 108$

Small triangle: $\frac{1}{2} \times 9 \times 9 = 40.5$

Large triangle: $\frac{1}{2} \times 21 \times 21 = 220.5$

Total area = $369\,\text{cm}^2$

b Area of the original sheet is $21 \times 30 = 630\,\text{cm}^2$

The fraction is $\dfrac{369}{630} = \dfrac{41}{70}$

10

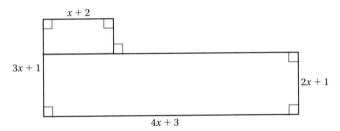

a The area is $x(x + 2) + (2x + 1)(4x + 3)$

$9x^2 + 12x + 3$

b $x = 5$

c $9 \times 5^2 + 12 \times 5 + 3 = 288\,\text{m}^2$

d The perimeter $= 14x + 8$. When $x = 5$ the perimeter is $14 \times 5 + 8 = 78\,\text{m}$. Therefore 78 posts are needed.

e $78 \times 3 = 234\,\text{m}$ of wire

f $78 \times 18.5 + 234 \times 2.30 = £1981.20$

Draw a good diagram and then work out the lengths of the sides.

Now there is enough information to work out the areas.

Either work out the area of the rectangle and the two triangles and add them, or work out the area of the original sheet of paper and subtract the two triangles.

You can't work out the area of the shape immediately, but you can work it out by working out separately the area of the rectangles in it. There are several ways to divide up the shape. The diagram shows one.

Expand brackets and collect like terms

$4 \times 4 \times 4 = 64 \, \text{cm}^2$

Two cubes have a volume of $128 \, \text{cm}^2$.

The volume of the extra water is: $\pi r^2 h$

The radius is 4 cm, so:

$\pi \times 4^2 \times h = 128$

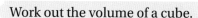 Work out the volume of a cube.

When two cubes are dropped into the cylinder, the water level goes up. The increase in volume is the same as the volume of the cubes.

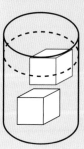

$h = 2.6 \, \text{cm} \, (1 \, \text{d.p.})$

 a

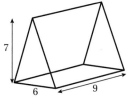

First, draw and label a diagram.

The area of the triangular cross-section is $\frac{1}{2} \times 6 \times 7$
$= 21 \, \text{cm}^2$

The volume of the prism is $21 \times 9 = 189 \, \text{cm}^3$

b The volume of the pentagonal prism is $9 \times L = 216$

$L = 189 \div 9 = 21 \, \text{cm}$

You could start by working out the volume of a cylinder of water than is 11 cm high.

Volume of cylinder $= \pi \times 3^2 \times 11 = 311.01767\ldots \, \text{cm}^3$

Volume of water (a cylinder) = area of circular base × height

$311 \, \text{cm}^3 = 311 \, \text{ml}$

Volume of water (in ml)

$500 \, \text{ml} - 311.01767 \, \text{ml} = 189 \, \text{ml} \, (3 \, \text{s.f.})$

Volume of water left in bottle

A	7. Total number of sixes is 7. Relative frequency is 0.7
B	4. Total number of sixes is 11. Relative frequency is 0.65
C	3. Total number of sixes is 14. Relative frequency is 0.47
D	6. Total number of sixes is 20. Relative frequency is 0.5
E	4. Total number of sixes is 24. Relative frequency is 0.48
	... and so on

After 10 students have taken their throws there are 44 sixes and the relative frequency is 0.44.

After 15 students have taken their throws there are 68 sixes and the relative frequency is 0.45.

After 20 students have taken their throws there are 83 sixes and the relative frequency is 0.415.

The relative frequency is going up and down, but it looks as if it is settling somewhere close to 0.4.

As more trials are done the relative frequency is generally closer to the actual value, so the actual value of the probability is probably about 0.4. This means that the dice is a biased one.

It probably makes sense to start working out the probability after each student has had a go.

Now you might want to skip a few.

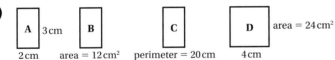

A and D are similar because the lengths of the sides of D are twice those of A.

B and C are not similar.

Start by drawing all the shapes.

You know all about A.

B could have dimensions 2 × 6 or 3 × 4

C could have dimensions 1 × 9, 2 × 8, 3 × 7 or 4 × 6

D has a length of 4 cm and must have a height of 6 cm.

16 **a** 7 × £4.20 = £29.40

Start with the total cost of the equipment.

(it will be higher than this because we don't know how much the drinks and snacks will cost)

$6x + 20 \geqslant 29.40$

There are six friends and they will each pay the same amount. Daniel has £20.

b $6x + 20 \geqslant 29.40$ means that $x \geqslant 1.566666...$

They must pay at least £1.56 each.

17 **a** 40 × 30 = 1200 unit squares

Start by working out the area of the rectangle.

$\frac{4}{5}$ of 1200 = 960

Now you can work out the shaded area.

You want to have $\frac{5}{6}$ of 1200 = 1000 shaded, so you need to shade an extra 40 unit squares.

b 960 is shaded from the first rectangle.

$\frac{2}{3}$ of 1200 = 800 is shaded from the second rectangle.

One way to do this is to work out the total area and the total amount that is shaded.

The fraction of the whole thing that is shaded is:

$$\frac{930 + 800}{1200 + 1200} = \frac{1760}{2400} = \frac{11}{15}$$

c $\frac{3}{4}$ of 2400 = 1800, so an extra 40 unit squares need to be shaded.

You already know that 1760 unit squares are shaded.

a $220\,\text{cm} = \pi \times d$

Circumference $= \pi \times$ diameter d

$d = 220\,\text{cm} \div \pi = 70.02817\ldots\,\text{cm}$

Use inverse operations to find the value of d.

Javed's tyre has a diameter of 70 cm

b $50 \times 220\,\text{cm} = 11000\,\text{cm} = 110\,\text{m}$

When the wheels go round once the bicycle will travel the length of the circumference.

c $600\,\text{m} + 550\,\text{m} + 900\,\text{m} + 550\,\text{m} + 200\,\text{m} + 350\,\text{m} + 270\,\text{m} + 150\,\text{m} + 170\,\text{m} + 200\,\text{m} = 3940\,\text{m}$

Calculate the missing lengths on the diagram.

$3940\,\text{m} \div 2.2\,\text{m} = 1790.90909\ldots$

1791 revolutions

This is the number of revolutions to the nearest whole number.

 a $4x + 6y = 9.20$

Let x be the number of cups of tea and y be the number of cupcakes.

b $5x + 2y = 7.10$

c $4x + 6y = 9.20$

$15x + 6y = 21.30$ (multiply the second equation by 3)

Solve for x.

$11x = 12.10$ (subtract the first equation from the second one)

Substitute for x.

$x = 1.10$ (tea costs £1.10)

$4 \times 1.10 + 6y = 9.20$

$6y = 4.80$

$y = 0.80$ (a cupcake costs £0.80)

121

20 **a** In a regular shape all the angles must be the same so working these out might be a good starting point.

The angles in a regular hexagon are 120°, and those in a regular pentagon are 108°.

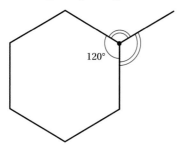

The angles around a point should add up to 360°, but here they make 336°, so they don't fit the pattern of the quilt.

b 3 × 120° = 360°, so regular hexagons will fit around the edge. Equilateral triangles would also fit:

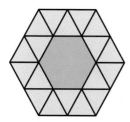

c A regular decagon can be surrounded by regular pentagons.

The interior angle of a regular pentagon is 108°.

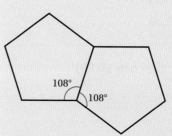

So two regular pentagons have angles of 108 + 108 = 216°. This leaves 360° – 216° = 144°

You now have to identify the regular polygon that has an interior angle of 144°.

The exterior angle is 180 – 144 = 36

Exterior angles always sum to 360°, so there must be 10 of them and the shape must have 10 sides.

1 **a**

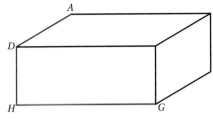

5 + 6 + 20 = 31 cm

Adding the ant's route to a copy of the diagram might help.

b

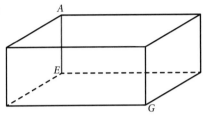

There are several different ways to go via E. The quickest ones still involve using 5, 6 and 20 = 31 cm

c

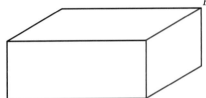

The smallest route is around the smallest rectangle:
5 + 6 + 5 + 6 = 22 cm

d

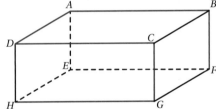

$B \to A \to D \to C \to G \to H \to E \to F \to B$ gives a length of 102 cm

It is not possible to go along every edge, so use the longest edges as much as possible.

2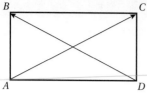

Using the algebra: $\overrightarrow{AC} = a + b$

$\overrightarrow{DB} = b - a$

Although the diagonals of the rectangle are equal in length, the vectors are going in different direction so the vectors are not equal.

3 **a**

The red lines on the diagram show that you need 180° plus a third of 180° (60°), which is 240° in total.

b When the minute hand makes a full turn the hour hand moves one hour, which means the hour hand moves at $\frac{1}{12}$ of the speed.

$\frac{1}{12}$ of 240° = 20°

4 **a**

The length of the fence is:

$\pi \times 17 = 53.407075 \ldots$ m

53.4 m

A copy of the diagram with the extra line added will help.

Circumference of circle = $\pi \times$ diameter

Round the answer to 3 s.f.

b

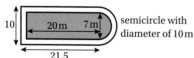

semicircle with diameter of 10 m

Length of fence:
21.5 + 10 + 21.5 + semicircle with diameter of 10 m

Semicircle:
$\pi \times 10 \div 2$

Total length is 68.7 m

68.7 m – 53.4 m = 15.3 m

Calculate the difference in lengths of fencing.

Ian will need to buy 15.3 m more fencing than Gerry.

Conclusion.

5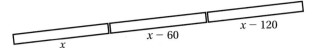

The total length is $x + x{-}60 + x{-}120$, which is $3x - 180$.

This is equal to 5.1 m, which is 510 cm.

$3x - 180 = 510$

$3x = 690$

$x = 230\,\text{cm}$

Sections are 230 cm, 170 cm and 110 cm.

Draw a diagram of the three sections of the ladder, with the numbers in cm.

---

6 Length of $AB = 2$

Length of $EF = 1$

Scale factor $= \dfrac{1}{2}$

Length of $BC = 6$

Length of $FG = \dfrac{1}{2} \times 6 = 3$

G: (1.5, 2.5) and H: (0.5, 2.5)

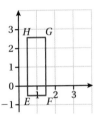

Read off the lengths AB and EF.

Calculate the scale factor of $ABCD$ to $EFGH$.

Use the scale factor to calculate the length FG (corresponding to BC).

Drawing this onto a copy of the diagram will help.

---

7 Right-hand triangle:

$180 - (30 + 90) = 60°$

Left-hand triangle:

$180 - (60 + 90) = 30°$

The two triangles are identical because they are congruent, by ASA.

This time the useful idea is actually to find the missing angles of the triangles.

Use the fact that angles in a triangle sum to 180°.

This means they must have the same area and you don't need to work out the two areas (which are 36.6mm² to 3 s.f).

8 **a**

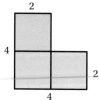

Divide the area into congruent shapes. Congruent shapes have the same area, so you could start by working out the area of the original diagram, which is 12 square units.

To have three congruent shapes the area of each one must be 4 square units. An easy way to make an area of 4 is to have a square.

b

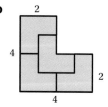

To make four congruent shapes the area of each one must be 3 square units. If you try to use straight lines it doesn't work, either with rectangles or with triangles. There are other shapes that have an area of 3 square units, and these will work here.

9

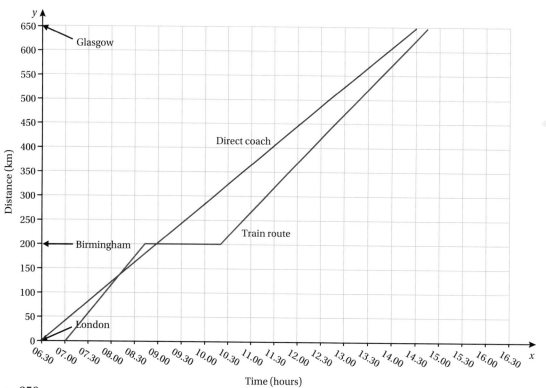

Time (hours)

Even though the question doesn't ask you to draw a graph, it is helpful to draw one. Note that the graph shows 'average speeds' as the actual speeds will vary during the journeys.

a $\dfrac{650}{8} = 81.25$ km/h

b 7 h 40 min is $7\frac{2}{3}$ h

$650 \div 7\frac{2}{3} = 84.8$ km/h

10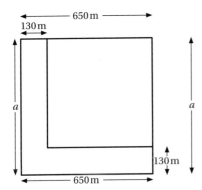

Add some lines to make it into a rectangle.

This makes it easy to see that the perimeter of the shape (which is the same as the perimeter of the rectangle) is $a + a + 650 + 650 = 2a + 1300$

This is the same as 2.28 km, so (after converting that to 2280 m) you can make an equation:

$2a + 1300 = 2280$

Solving this gives $a = 490$ m, so the value of a required is 0.49 km.

Make sure you answer in the units asked for.

11

This diagram has extra lines on it.

It shows that $\frac{9}{16}$ of the diagram is purple.

Team **A** have given an area rather than a proportion. 0 marks

Team **B** have got the wrong fraction. Maybe they saw that $\frac{3}{4}$ of this part was shaded:

But that is not the whole thing.   0 or 1 mark

Team **C** are correct. Maybe they used the idea that the inner big white triangle is not included (leaving $\frac{3}{4}$ of the whole diagram) and then $\frac{3}{4}$ of that is shaded, which is $\frac{3}{4} \times \frac{3}{4}$. This equals $\frac{9}{16}$.   4 marks

Team **D** are correct. $\frac{9}{16} = 0.5625$.   4 marks

12 Area of the classic pizza = $\pi \times 6^2$

$= 113.0973\ldots$ inches^2

The area of the rustic pizza is a rectangle of 7×11 plus a circle (two semicircles) of radius 3.5 inches.

Work out the area of the classic pizza.

Work out the area of the rustic pizza.

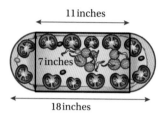

11 inches

7 inches

18 inches

Area = $7 \times 11 + \pi \times 3.5^2$

$= 115.4845\ldots$ inches^2

You do get a little more for your money when you buy the rustic pizza. The area is approximately 2 inches^2 larger than the classic pizza.

Conclusion.

13

This is a hard question. A well-labelled diagram might help

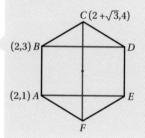

$C\,(2+\sqrt{3},4)$

$(2,3)\,B$ D

$(2,1)\,A$ E

F

a $\overrightarrow{DE}$ is the *same* vector as $\overrightarrow{BA}$. This is $\begin{pmatrix}0\\-2\end{pmatrix}$ (the same numbers as $\overrightarrow{AB}$ but with the opposite sign).

b To get from B to C you need to go right by $\sqrt{3}$ and up by 1, so the vector $\overrightarrow{BC} = \begin{pmatrix}\sqrt{3}\\1\end{pmatrix}$

c F is immediately below C. C is 1 above B, so F must be 1 below A, which means the distance from F to C is 4. The vector $\overrightarrow{FC} = \begin{pmatrix}0\\4\end{pmatrix}$.

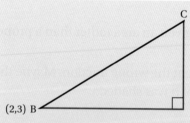

C

$(2,3)\,B$

In this triangle the marked angle is 60° and the length of BC is 2. Use trigonometry to work out that the horizontal distance is and that the vertical distance is .

d The vector $\overrightarrow{AE}$ is the same as the vector $\overrightarrow{BD}$. D is level with B, so you just need to look at how far D is to the right of B. To get from B to C you go right by $\sqrt{3}$, so you need to double this.

The vector $\overrightarrow{AE} = \begin{pmatrix} 2\sqrt{3} \\ 0 \end{pmatrix}$

e The vector $\overrightarrow{AC}$ is the same as $\overrightarrow{AB} + \overrightarrow{BC}$. This is

$$\begin{pmatrix} 0 \\ 2 \end{pmatrix} + \begin{pmatrix} \sqrt{3} \\ 1 \end{pmatrix} = \begin{pmatrix} \sqrt{3} \\ 3 \end{pmatrix}$$

f $\overrightarrow{EF}$ is the same vector as $\overrightarrow{CB}$. This is $\begin{pmatrix} -\sqrt{3} \\ -1 \end{pmatrix}$ (the same numbers as $\overrightarrow{BC}$ but with the opposite sign).

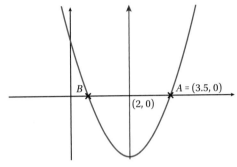

The coordinates of point B are $(0.5, 0)$.

C is $(3.5, 0)$ and D is $(0.5, 0)$.

The question says that the graph is symmetrical about the line $x = 2$, so it makes sense to draw that line in.

Now you can see that the crossing value for point A is 1.5 to the right of the line of reflection, so point B must cross at 1.5 to the left of the line.

In the second diagram the quadratic has been reflected in the x-axis so the crossing points are the same.

15 **a**

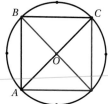

The inner shape is a square, so the angle *ABC* is 90°

Here are some changes to the diagram that make it easier to see what is going on.

b

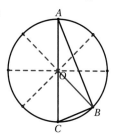

The extra lines show that there are 8 equal angles around the centre of the circle.

Each angle is therefore 360° ÷ 8 = 45°

Triangle *OCB* is isosceles, which means angles *B* and *C* are equal and add up to 135°. Each one is therefore 67.5°.

Triangle *OAB* is also isosceles and the angle *AOB* = 135° (three lots of 45°). Angles *A* and *B* are equal and add up to 45°, so each one is 22.5°.

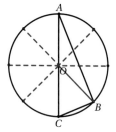

Angle *ABC* is 67.5° + 22.5° = 90°

c

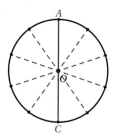

The angles around the centre are all 36° (360° ÷ 10). When you choose a point for *B* you will make isosceles triangles and can work out the other angles as in part **c**.

16   **a**   3.6 m = 360 cm

     360 cm ÷ 18 cm = 20 stairs in the staircase.

The stairs must cover a vertical distance of 3.6 m. Each step is 18 cm high.

b   Base length of staircase = 20 × 28 cm = 560 cm

$$a^2 + b^2 = c^2$$

$$560^2 + 360^2 = c^2$$

$$443200 = c^2$$

$$c = 665.73... \text{ cm}$$

The banister rail will go diagonally up the stairs. It will need to be the same length as the diagonal length of the staircase. Use Pythagoras' theorem to calculate this.

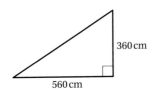

The banister rail will need to be 6.66 m in length (to the nearest cm).

17   **a**   If the students are looking up at an angle of 45°, then they create a right-angled, isosceles triangle. (Isosceles because if one angle is 90° and another is 45° then the remaining angle will also be 45°.)

Assuming that the student's height is small compared to the height of the tree, then the horizontal distance along the ground is approximately the same as the height of the tree (two equal sides in an isosceles triangle).

A good diagram will help.

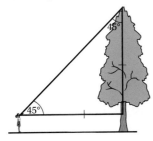

b

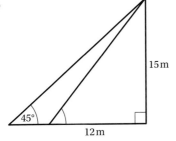

Opposite side = height of tree = 15 m

Adjacent side = 12 m

Guy's angle = $\tan^{-1} \dfrac{15}{12} = 51.34 ...°$

Guy's angle is approximately 51°.

1 a $1 \times 7, 2 \times 7, 3 \times 7, 4 \times 7, 5 \times 7, 6 \times 7 \dots$

7, 14, 21,   28,   35, 42 …

$35 - 10 = 25$

Jamie's initial number was 5.

Let Jamie's number be x.

$7x = 10 = 25$

$7x = 25 + 10$

$7x = 35$

b $1 \times 4, 2 \times 4, 3 \times 4, 4 \times 4, 5 \times 4, 6 \times 4 \dots$

4, 8, 12, 16, **20**, 24 …

$11 + 9 = 20$

Simon's initial number was 11.

Let Simon's number be y

$$\frac{(y + 9)}{4} = 5$$

$(y + 9) = 20$

$y = 20 - 9$

To solve a simpler problem think about just multiplying by 7 (forget about subtracting 10, at least initially). So inspect multiples of 7.

Now think about subtracting 10.

$5 \times 7 = 35$

This simplification allows us to see inside the problem. Now move to a more efficient approach.

Simon's number is 11. To solve a simpler problem think about just multiplying by 4.

Now add the 9.

Now move to a more efficient approach.

2

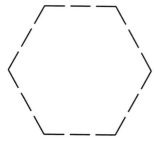

Each panel is $10.8 \div 18 = 0.6\,\text{m}$.

You could start by drawing a diagram.

You can see that there are 18 panels and that the total perimeter is 10.8 m.

3 **a** To start with, I am going to ignore the measurements on the cubes. If I have a box like this:

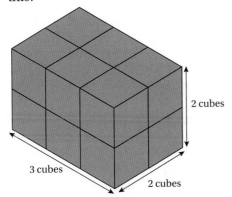

it will hold 2 × 2 × 3 = 12 cubes.

This tells me that I need 3 numbers that multiply together to make 40.

There are several ways of packing the cubes, which include:

4 × 2 × 5 (8 (4 × 2) cubes in each of 5 layers)

5 × 2 × 4 (10 (5 × 2) cubes in each of 4 layers)

8 × 1 × 5 (8 (8 × 1) cubes in each of 5 layers)

2 × 2 × 10 (4 (2 × 2) cubes in each of 10 layers)

b The first of these looks like this:

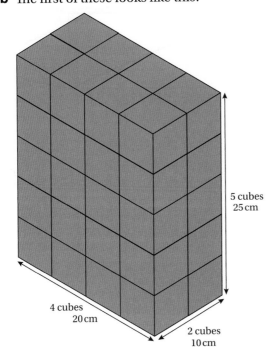

4 a $4^3 = 4 \times 4 \times 4 =$ even

$3^4 = 3 \times 3 \times 3 \times 3 =$ odd

Even + odd = odd

So $4^3 + 3^4 =$ odd

b $6^7 =$ even

$3^7 =$ odd

So $6^7 + 3^7 =$ odd

Think about what happens when you add odd and even numbers.

Show that:

Even + even = even

Odd + odd = even

Even + odd = odd

Then do the same for multiplication:

Even × even = even

Odd × odd = odd

Even × even × even... = even

Odd × odd × odd... = odd

An even number raised to any power is even

$(\text{even})^x =$ even

An odd number raised to any power is odd

$(\text{odd})^x =$ odd

5 a The diagram shows two wedges. That means 20 of these pairs total a metre long, so x must be 5 cm.

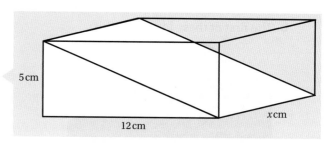

b To make £30 profit and cover the cost of the wood (£5), Ahmed has to take at least £35.

As he has 40 wedges to sell, the minimum cost to achieve this is £35 ÷ 40 = 87.5p.

This rounds to 88p.

6 **a** Percentage decrease = $0.60 \div 7.60 \times 100$

   = 7.89%

The discount on each adult ticket is £0.60.

b Percentage decrease = $0.45 \div 3.40 \times 100$

   = 13.2%

The discount on each child ticket is £0.45.

c £7.60 + £3.40 = £11.00

There are the same number of adults as children, so work out the cost of 1 adult and 1 child ticket on a normal day.

£7.00 + £2.95 = £9.95

Work out the cost of 1 adult and 1 child ticket on a Thursday.

$1.05 \div 11.00 \times 100 = 9.55\%$

Work out the percentage loss.

7 $\dfrac{9}{10} \times \dfrac{3}{4} \times \dfrac{1}{3} = \dfrac{27}{120} = \dfrac{9}{40}$

Work out the probability of not stopping at each point.

8

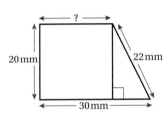

Make this simpler by focusing on the right-angled triangle first.

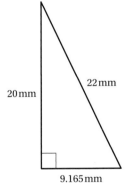

Use Pythagoras' theorem to work out the base of this triangle.

The distance across the top of the trapezium is therefore 30 – 9.165 = 20.8 mm (3 s.f.)

9

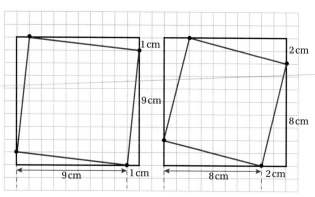

Label what you know. Use the squares on the paper to find the lengths.

$a^2 + b^2 = c^2$ $a^2 + b^2 = c^2$

$9^2 + 1^2 = c^2$ $8^2 + 2^2 = c^2$

$82 = c^2$ $68 = c^2$

$c = \sqrt{82} = 9.055...\text{cm}$ $c = \sqrt{68} = 8.246...\text{cm}$

A line in the first logo is longer than a line in the second logo, so the total line length of the first logo is greater.

Now focus on a triangle. Use Pythagoras' theorem to calculate the side length of the tilted square.

10 **a**

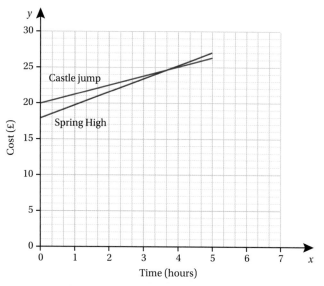

Spring High: (0, 18), (5, 27)

b £27

c See graph above.

Castle Jump: (0, 20), (5, 26.50)

d approx 3.5 hours

11 100 000 0 ÷ 60 = 16 666.666... minutes

16 666.666... ÷ 60 = 277.777... hours

277.777... ÷ 24 = 11.574 days

Some numbers will be much quicker to say than others. It is quick to say 'three' or 'five hundred thousand', but it takes much longer to say 'two hundred and twenty-two thousand, two hundred and twenty-two'. If each number takes about 2 seconds to say (on average), then it will take about 23 days to say them all.

Even allowing for breaks for sleeping and eating, you could easily do this in your lifetime.

> This method starts by working out how many days is the same as 1 million seconds.

12

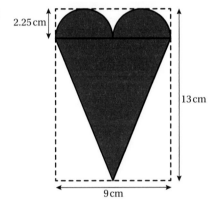

The two semicircles make a circle, radius 2.25 cm.

Area of circle = $\pi \times 2.25^2 = 15.9043 \ldots$ cm²

Height of triangle = $13 - 2.25 = 10.75$ cm

Area of triangle = $\frac{1}{2} \times 9 \times 10.75 = 48.375$ cm²

$9 \times 13 - 15.9043 - 48.375 = 52.7$ cm² (3 s.f.)

> Start by working out the areas of the different parts of the heart.

> Subtract the areas of the circle and triangle from the area of the rectangle.

a Principal × 1.08^{10}

= Principal × 2.16

Yes, he would more than double his money.

b £40 000 × 1.08^{10}

£86 357 to the nearest pound

c £30 000 × 1.08^{10} = £64 767.75

£31 000 × 1.08^{10} = £66 926.67

£32 000 × 1.08^{10} = £69 085.60

£33 000 × 1.08^{10} = £71 244.52

£34 000 × 1.08^{10} = £73 403.45

£35 000 × 1.08^{10} = £75 572.37

 a $140 \div 1\frac{1}{2} = 93.3 \, \text{km/h}$

b $140 \div 1\frac{1}{3} = 105 \, \text{km/h}$

c 10 minutes

d 12 noon

e 4.5 hours, 62.2 km/h

f 3 hours 40 minutes, 76.36 km/h

g 105 km/h is only 65.6 miles per hour, so no one was speeding at any point as long as the speed limit was 70 mph.

1 **a** When you add numbers the order is not important.
Both answers are $1\frac{1}{3}$

b When you carry out a subtraction the order is important. $1 - \frac{1}{3} = \frac{2}{3}$ but $\frac{1}{3} - 1 = -\frac{2}{3}$
Notice that the only difference between the two subtraction answers is the negative symbol.

2 **i** You could:

multiply $\frac{1}{4}$ by anything bigger than 2

divide $\frac{1}{4}$ by anything between 0 and $\frac{1}{2}$

add anything bigger than $\frac{1}{4}$ or subtract anything less than $\frac{(-1)}{4}$ to $\frac{1}{4}$.

> Note: many solutions to this problem are possible. These are some solutions to part **i**.

3 **a** e.g. $\frac{1}{50}, \frac{1}{49}, \frac{1}{48}, \frac{1}{47}, \frac{1}{46}$

> This question can be answered in many ways, but making changes to the original set of fractions works well.

b e.g. $\frac{2}{6}, \frac{2}{5}, \frac{2}{4}, \frac{2}{3}, \frac{2}{2}$

c e.g. $\frac{6}{2}, \frac{7}{2}, \frac{8}{2}, \frac{9}{2}, \frac{10}{2}$

or

$\frac{5}{3}, \frac{7}{4}, \frac{9}{5}, \frac{8}{3}, \frac{9}{2}$

> You could sprinkle some unrelated fractions around (such as in this final example), but it is easier to work in a systematic way and to make use of some patterns.

4 To 1 significant figure this calculation is:

$20 \times 800 = 16\,000$, which is about 10 times the size of 1903.02. The answer is likely to be incorrect.

Start with $23.64 \times 805 = 1903.02$

If $23.64 \times 805 = 1903.02$ is true, then:

$2.364 \times 805 = 190.302$

and $2.364 \times 8.05 = 1.90\,302$

The left-hand side must be bigger than 16, so the calculation can't be correct.

5 **a** $400 \, \text{mg} = 0.4 \, \text{g}$
$400 \, \text{g} + 400 \, \text{mg} = 400.4 \, \text{g}$

$0.5 \, \text{kg} = 500 \, \text{g}$
$0.5 \, \text{kg} - 90 \, \text{g} = 410 \, \text{g}$

$400 \, \text{g} + 400 \, \text{mg} < 0.5 \, \text{kg} - 90 \, \text{g}$

Change the quantities so they use the same units. It makes sense to work in grams. $1 \, \text{kg} = 1000 \, \text{g}$ and $1 \, \text{g} = 1000 \, \text{mg}$

b $0.1 \, \text{km} = 100 \, \text{m}$
$150 \, \text{cm} = 1.5 \, \text{m}$
$0.1 \, \text{km} + 150 \, \text{cm} = 101.5 \, \text{m}$

$900 \, \text{cm} = 9 \, \text{m}$
$110 \, \text{m} - 900 \, \text{cm} = 101 \, \text{m}$

$0.1 \, \text{km} + 150 \, \text{cm} > 110 \, \text{m} - 900 \, \text{cm}$

Convert everything to metres. $1 \, \text{km} = 1000 \, \text{m}$ and $1 \, \text{m} = 100 \, \text{cm}$

c 0.75 hours = 45 minutes
600 seconds = 10 minutes
0.75 hours + 600 seconds = 55 minutes

0.1 hours = 6 minutes
50 minutes + 0.1 hours = 56 minutes

0.75 hours + 600 seconds < 50 minutes + 0.1 hours

Convert everything to minutes.

6 **a** $1 - (0.2 + 0.7) = 0.1$

Change $\frac{1}{5}$ into 0.2

b $0.7 \times 140 = 98$

c The number of bulbs that grow =
$\frac{6}{7} \times 140 = 120$

The number of those bulbs that are red =
$\frac{1}{5} \times 120 = 24$

Snail 1: 36 000 mm/h (÷ 10)

3600 cm/h (÷ 60)

60 cm/min (÷ 60)

1 cm/s

Snail 2: 0.01 m/s (× 100)

1 cm/s

Snail 3: 5 km/day (× 1000)

5000 m/day (× 100)

500 000 cm/day (÷ 24)

20 833.333... cm/h (÷ 60)

347.222... cm/min (÷ 60)

5.787... cm/s (=5.8 cm/s to 1 d.p.)

Snail 4: 700 cm/h (÷ 60)

11.666... cm/min (÷ 60)

0.19444... cm/s (=0.2 cm/s to 1 d.p.)

Snail **3** finishes first.

> To compare the snails' speeds they must be measured in the same units.
>
> In this question it might be sensible to convert all the speeds into cm per second (cm/s).

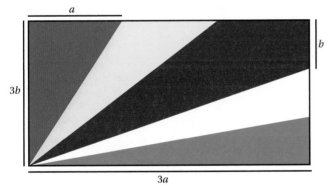

> Label the triangles.
>
> Across the top of the flag each triangle has a side that is a, which means the whole flag has a width of $3a$. On the right, each triangle has a side that is b, which means the whole flag has a height of $3b$.

The area of the white triangle is $\frac{1}{2} \times b \times 3a = \frac{1}{2} \times 3ab$

The area of the blue triangle is $\frac{1}{2} \times a \times 3b = \frac{1}{2} 3ab$

This shows that the two areas are the same.

> Now use the formula for the area of a triangle.

9   **a** $1 + 2 + 3 = 6$, which is 2×3

$2 + 3 + 4 = 9$, which is 3×3

$3 + 4 + 5 = 12$, which is 4×3

$(n - 1) + (n) + (n + 1)$

$n - 1 + n + n + 1 = 3n$

Yes, this is true for all integers.

b $n + (n + 1) + (n + 2) + (n + 3) = 4n + 6$

c

Number of numbers	Formula, based on the first number being n
2	$2n + 1$
3	$3n + 3$
4	$4n + 6$
5	$5n + 10$
6	$6n + 15$
7	$7n + 21$
8	$8n + 28$

First, try it out with some more sets of three consecutive integers. You could work systematically.

Once you are convinced that it works, try to think about why.

There are several different ways of explaining this. To start with, think about a general set of three consecutive numbers.

Using algebra you can simplify this expression.

The expression simplifies to $3n$ ($3 \times$ the middle number). So it must be true for all integers.

You could do this algebraically, where n is the first number.

The method for part **b** can be extended for any number of numbers.

a $430 \div 142 = 3.028\,169...$

   $400 \div 142 = 2.816\,901...$

   $250 \div 142 = 1.760\,563...$

   $430 \div 125 = 3.44$

   $400 \div 125 = 3.2$

   $250 \div 125 = 2$

   $430 \div 10 = 43$

   $400 \div 10 = 40$

   $250 \div 10 = 25$

   She can fit $3 \times 2 \times 40$ CD cases into the packing box.

   240 CDs will fit into each box.

b 2

Start by considering the different ways in which the CDs could be arranged.

Check whether 142 mm will divide into 43 cm, 40 cm, 25 cm.

Check whether 125 mm will divide into 43 cm, 40 cm, 25 cm.

Check whether 10 mm will divide into 43 cm, 40 cm, 25 cm.

The answers in bold give the smallest error while using all the dimensions of the box and the CD

Look for best fits.

$430 \div 142 = 3.028\,169...$

$250 \div 125 = 2$

$400 \div 10 = 40$

a Translations of $\begin{pmatrix} 0 \\ a \end{pmatrix}$

   Where a is any number: positive, negative or zero.

b Translation of $\begin{pmatrix} b \\ b \end{pmatrix}$

   Where b is any number: positive, negative or zero.

Daisy's shape can move up or down. This means the x-coordinate stays the same but the y-coordinate can vary.

For the shape to stay on the line $y = x$, it must move up and right by the same amount.

The perimeter of the semicircle is $\pi \times \dfrac{6}{2} = 9.42...$ cm

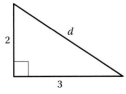

$a^2 = 2^2 + 3^2$

$d = \sqrt{13} = 3.605\,55...$ cm

$\pi \times 3.60655...$ cm $= 11.327...$ cm

Circumference $= \pi \times 3.606\,55...$ cm $= 11.327...$ cm

Total perimeter $= 9.42... + 11.327... = 20.7$ cm (3 s.f.)

Treat this as a large semicircle and a smaller circle.

Now find the diameter of the smaller circle.

This is the hypotenuse of a right-angled triangle.

a 1 Try a different starting shape.

2 Try a different pair of perpendicular mirror lines.

3 Try a different starting position for the shape.

b

Mirror line 1

Mirror line 2

Mikey has looked at one example and drawn his conclusion based on this.

If you carry out the reflection in Mikey's chosen mirror lines ($y = 0$ and $x = 0$) with this new shape it becomes clear that something else is happening – the shape has been rotated 180° about the origin.

Because Mikey's original shape was a rectangle, it has rotational symmetry and he therefore did not notice that the rotation had happened.

His conclusion was not incorrect, but it was not the full answer. That depends on the nature of the starting shape.

1 **a** 1.099 and 1.308   both start with 1.

   1.099 and 1.308   in the tenths position 3 is bigger than 0, so 1.308 is bigger than 1.099

   b 0.5 is equal to 0.50 and 0.500, so 0.5 = 0.500

   c 1.7 and 1.534   both start with 1.

   1.7 and 1.534   in the tenths position 7 is bigger than 5, so 1.7 is bigger than 1.534.

Use your knowledge of place value in this question.

---

2 $2x - 1 + 2x - 1 + x + 3 = 41$

   $5x + 1 = 41$

   This gives $x = 8$, so the sides are 11 cm, 15 cm, 15 cm.

It is common to write an equation for the perimeter of the triangle and then to solve it.

You can check your answer by confirming that these lengths add up to 41.

---

3 Method 1: For a rough approximation you could estimate the length of one of the fingers in the large handprint, and then compare this with the same finger in the small handprint.

Method 2: Count the whole squares inside the large handprint. Match up the part squares, to see how many whole squares you can make. Find the total. Do the same for the small handprint. Find the difference.

The area of the large handprint is four times the area of the small handprint.

This is a question about area. Here are two methods you could use to estimate the area.

---

4 **a** Ratio of water : sugar solution : lemon juice

   2500 : 500 : 750

   250 : 50 : 75

   10 : 2 : 3

   b 2500 + 500 + 750 = 3750

   = 3.75 litres

   c 10 : 1 : 3

   d 2500 + 250 + 750 = 3500

   = 3.5 litres

Here you need to convert the quantities so they are all in the same units.

Start with the ratio in part **a** and then halve the sugar solution.

5 **a** $\frac{3}{6} = \frac{1}{2}$

> Use what you know about the properties of numbers.

> The multiples of 2 on a dice are 2, 4 and 6.

b $\frac{2}{6} = \frac{1}{3}$

> The square numbers on a dice are 1 and 4.

c $\frac{2}{6} = \frac{1}{3}$

> The numbers greater than 4 are 5 and 6.

d $\frac{3}{6} = \frac{1}{2}$

> The prime numbers on a dice are 2, 3 and 5.

e 0

> There is no number 9.

6 **a** $\frac{4}{30} = \frac{2}{15}$

> 4 yellow balls and 30 balls in total

b $4 \times 5 = 20$

c $\frac{2}{15}$

> This is the same as the answer to part **a**. A ball chosen at random (to be first or to be furthest), has a probability of $\frac{2}{15}$ of being yellow).

7

> In this question rounding, upper and lower bounds are needed.

a The smallest the population could be is 6.5 billion.

> The number 7 has been obtained by rounding to the nearest whole number (of billions).

> This means that the actual number could have been rounded up to 7. For example, 6.9 would round up to 7, and so would 6.6. In fact as long as the number was 6.5 or greater then it would round up to 7.

b The largest the population could be is just less than 7.5 billion. (7.5 billion would round up to 8 billion.) 7.5 billion is the upper bound.

c The population, p, is greater than or equal to 6.5 billion and is less than 7.5 billion.

Where p is the population of the Earth:

$6\,500\,000\,000 \leqslant p < 7\,500\,000\,000$

d If it has been rounded to the nearest billion then it can vary by almost a billion.

8

a $t + 15$

Let t be the cost of a jam doughnut in pence. The iced doughnut is 15 more than this.

b £17.70

This is similar to other questions involving writing expressions and equations.

$3t + 5(t + 15) = 1195$

$3t + 5t + 75 = 1195$

$8t = 1195 - 75$

$8t = 1120$

$t = 1120 \div 8 = 140$

$t = £1.40$, cost of iced doughnut = £1.55

If you get six of each then it will cost £1.40 × 6 + £1.55 × 6

9 a 225 minutes = 3 hours 45 minutes

A lot of information in the question is irrelevant. The carving time is the same for both birds. The turkey weighs 4.5 kg more, so it needs to be in the oven for 50 minutes × 4.5 longer.

b $t = 50m + 30$

c 5.5 kg

$5 \times 60 + 5 = 305$ minutes

$(305 - 30) \div 50$

d 9.25 am if no carving time is required.

9.05 am if 20 minutes of preparation time is needed.

10

Substitute the values given into the formula and see what happens.

a 34 m/s

$v = 22 + 0.4 \times 30$

$v = 34$

b 250 s

$50 = 0 + 0.2 \times t$

$t = 250$

c 52.5 m/s

$90 = u + 2.5 \times 15$

$u = 52.5$

11 Clearly this is a joke, but treat is as a question. Make some assumptions about Nick's 'normal' working hours. It might be sensible to assume a working day of 8 hours (9 am – 5 pm).

    a 5% of 8 hours is 0.4 of an hour. This doesn't mean very much, so change the 8 hours into minutes. Nick works 8 × 60 minutes = 480 minutes. 5% of this is 24 minutes.

    b One way to do this is to work out that on Wednesday it would be 40% of 480 mins (192 mins) and then to subtract 12% of 480 mins (57 mins and 36 seconds). Then subtract to get 134 mins and 24 seconds (2 hours 14 mins 24 seconds).

    c It might look as if it must be Nick because he works for 23% compared with Bernard's 18%, but if Bernard's working hours are longer then 18% of a larger amount could be bigger than 23% of something smaller.

> Calculate the amount of time spent working on Friday.

 12
    a Her son gets $\frac{1}{2}$, the first twin gets $\frac{1}{6}$ and the second twin gets $\frac{1}{6}$.

      The pet rescue centre gets $1 - \frac{1}{2} - \frac{1}{6} - \frac{1}{6} = \frac{1}{6}$.

    b $3:1:1:1$

    c Each daughter: $\frac{1}{6} \times £5\,000\,000$

      £833 000

    d $\frac{3}{5}$ remains, which is £3 million

      The children each get $\frac{1}{4} \times £3$ million $= £750\,000$

    e The remaining $\frac{1}{4}$ is shared between five grandchildren: £750 000 ÷ 5 = £150 000

    f £2 500 000 : £750 000

      10 : 3

> This is similar to the problems you have already solved in this question.

13 **a** turkey : chicken = 4 : 7 = 1 : 1.75

multiply by 6 to get 6 : 10.5

10.5 kg of chicken

b 250 g of herbs needed for 4 kg turkey

125 g needed for 2 kg turkey

250 + 125 = 375 g

c turkey : chicken

4 : 7

Multiply by 4 to get 16 : 28

16 kg of turkey

d herbs : turkey : chicken

250 : 4000 : 7000

1 : 16 : 28 (divide by 250)

Simplifying ratios is a useful idea here.

Change all quantities to grams.

14

This involves similar ideas to the previous question.

a 4800 Chelsea supporters

21 parts = 25 200 supporters

1 part = 25 200 divided by 21 = 1200

The number of Chelsea supporters = 1200 × 4

b 6000 children

4 adults : 1 child

One fifth of total attendance are children

Total = 25 200 + 4800 = 30 000

$\frac{1}{5}$ of 30 000 are children

c 18 000 more adults

30 000 – 6000 = 24 000 adults

24 000 – 6000 = 18 000 (adults – children)

d 2000 ice creams

$\frac{1}{3}$ of the children have ice creams

6000 ÷ 3

e 36 000 soft drinks

24 000 adults

Half of adults buy 3 soft drinks each

12 000 × 3

f 2000 : 36 000

1 : 18

ice cream : soft drinks

You could treat this as a question about proportionality.

a $320 = k(8 \times 10)$

$576 = k(12 \times 12)$

Charge $= 4 \times (12 \times 8)$

£384

Cost = constant of proportionality × area

$320 = 80k$

$k = 320 \div 80 = 4$

$576 = 144k$

$k = 576 \div 144 = 4$

Charge $= 4 \times$ area

4×96

b Any area measuring $140 \, \text{m}^2$

$14 \, \text{m} \times 10 \, \text{m}$

$7 \, \text{m} \times 20 \, \text{m}$

$5 \, \text{m} \times 28 \, \text{m}$

560 divide by 4 = area

a $\dfrac{2}{11}$

2 letter Ts in MATHEMATICS and 11 letters in total

b $\dfrac{2}{11} \times \dfrac{1}{10} = \dfrac{1}{55}$

if first card is T (probability $\dfrac{2}{11}$) there is one T left out of the 10 remaining cards

$a^2 + b^2 = c^2$

This is a Pythagoras question.

$32.3^2 + 57.7^2 = 4372.58$

but $80^2 = 6400$

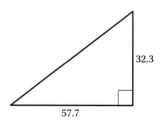

Jenny must have measured the diagonal incorrectly because Pythagoras' theorem doesn't work with her measurements. She has overestimated the diagonal length (which is actually 66.1 cm).

The TV is 26 inches.

2.54 cm = 1 inch

18 **a**

Husband		Son
8	57	
9 8 5	58	1 7 8 9 9
5 5	59	1 3 3 4
6 1	60	2 4
3 1	61	
3	62	

Key: 59|4 = 59.4 g

The stem and leaf diagram shows that there are fewer packets that weigh over 60 g than weigh less than 60 g.

> A stem and leaf diagram would be a good way to display the data.

b i and **ii** The median is 59.5 g for her husband and 59.1 g for her son.

c 59 g. The median weight for all packets is just over 59 g. 60 g is too high.

19

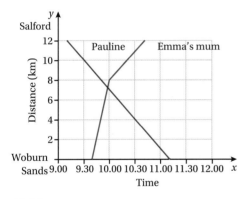

a 10.00

b 5 km

c 7 km

d 11.10

e 6 km/h

f 5 km

> It is useful to recognise that a travel graph is likely to help here.

> Draw a graph of the journeys.

> Use the graph to find how far Emma's mum is from Woburn Sands.

> Distance = 4 km
>
> Time = 40 minutes = $\frac{2}{3}$ hour
>
> Speed = $\frac{\text{distance}}{\text{time}}$

20 **a** 10 km

Read this off the graph.

   b 20 mins

The speed is the distance divided by the time, in this case 10 km divided by 20 minutes, which is 10 km divided by 0.33 hours = 30 km/h. 30 km/h is slow. There could be traffic congestion in Glasgow.

   c 2 stops, 20 minutes

Is there a place on the graph where time passes but the rider does not move?

   d Between 19.20 and 20.00 on the outward journey

The graph is steepest at this point.

   e 120 km/h

$$\text{Speed} = \frac{\text{distance}}{\text{time}}$$

   f 21.05

   g Approximately 26 km

   h 30 km/h

$$\text{Speed} = \frac{\text{distance}}{\text{time}} \text{ works here, as well.}$$

   i 60 km/h

21 **a**

In order to calculate the aspect ratio you need to know the height of Carlos' TV.

You know the diagonal length and the width so you need to apply Pythagoras' theorem.

Height = 17.6 inches = 18 inches (2 s.f.)

32 : 18

This simplifies to 16 : 9

   b

The aspect ratio of the TV is 16 : 9 (width : height)

We know the diagonal length so will have to apply Pythagoras' theorem.

$(9x)^2 + 256x^2 = 1764$

$337x^2 = 1764$

$x^2 = 1764 \div 337$

$x = \sqrt{1764 \div 337} = 2.287\ldots$ inches

Width = $16x = 16 \times 2.287\ldots = 36.6$ inches (to 1 d.p.)

Height = $9x = 9 \times 2.287\ldots = 20.6$ inches (to 1 d.p.)

22 **a** price = $k \div$ mileage

Use k as the constant of proportionality in an inverse proportion formula.

$2000 = k \div 10\,000$

$k = 2\,000\,000$

Price = $2\,000\,000 \div$ mileage

   b £1000

   c 5000 miles

1 Although this is a 3-day weekend, a usual weekend is 2 days so $\frac{1}{2}$ of that needs to be added. It is $\frac{1}{2}$ longer.

2 B is the best estimate (even though D is closest to the actual answer).

> A common way to estimate an answer is to round off the numbers in the question to 1 s.f.
>
> This would give $50 \times 20 \div 10 = 100$.

3 Kristie runs 10 miles each day, which is 16 km. Kristie is training a little more than Amar, but we don't know anything about the lengths of time they have been training, how fit they are generally, how old they are, whether they are doing other fitness work etc, so we can't really tell who is better prepared.

4

> The garden looks like a rectangle that is roughly 5 m by 12 m. This has an area of roughly 60 m², and at about £2 per square metre the turf would cost about £120 in total.

$7 \times 80\,\text{cm} = 560\,\text{cm}$ or $5.6\,\text{m}$

> Width of Nathan's garden

$5.6\,\text{m} \times 12\,\text{m} = 67.2\,\text{m}^2$

> Area of rectangle 5.6 m wide and 12 m long

1 paving slab $= 0.8\,\text{m} \times 0.8\,\text{m} = 0.64\,\text{m}^2$

Area of patio $= 15 \times 0.64\,\text{m}^2 = 9.6\,\text{m}^2$

> Area of triangular corner missing from top left

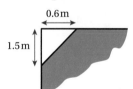

$\text{Area} = \frac{1}{2} \times 0.6\,\text{m} \times 1.5\,\text{m} = 0.45\,\text{m}^2$

Area of turf $= 67.2\,\text{m}^2 - 9.6\,\text{m}^2 - 0.45\,\text{m}^2 = 57.15\,\text{m}^2$, which is about 57 m²

The turf will cost $57 \times £2.34 = £133.38$

5

The field is roughly the same as this rectangle:

550 m

120 m

550 m is about 5 × 105 m, 120 m is about 2 × 68 m, so 10 football pitches will fit. This is about 20 acres, so 40 cows could be kept on the land.

The exact area is 550 × 90 + 270 × 60 = 65 700 m²

An acre is about 68 × 105 ÷ 2 = 3570 m²

The field is about 65700 ÷ 3570 = 18.4 acres

This is close to the initial estimate of 40.

18.4 × 2 = 36.8

So Rebecca could keep about 37 cows on this land.

6   **a**   Dark chocolate: 675 g

You need to convert a recipe for 8 people to a recipe that serves 20 people.

You could divide by 8 to find the ingredients for one serving and then multiply by 20.

Alternatively, you could multiply by $\frac{20}{8}$ (i.e $\frac{5}{2}$), which is the same as multiplying by $2\frac{1}{2}$.

  b   4 bars of 200 g each (because 3 bars is only 600 g)

  c   800 g – 675 g = 125 g

    675 : 125

    27 : 5

  d $\frac{3}{4}$ of 400 g is 300 g.

To serve 6 people you can divide by 8 and multiply by 6, or you can multiply by $\frac{6}{8}$, which is the same as $\frac{3}{4}$.

7 $\frac{45}{x} = \frac{6}{50}$

The fraction of the sample that has rings should be about the same as the fraction of the population that has rings.

6x = 45 × 50

6x = 2250

x = 375

There are 375 finches, so the keeper will need to find new homes for 25 of them.

8

a Idea 1: all the same age group – she should sample people of different ages.

Idea 2: likely to be generally fit anyway as they are involved in sport. Should sample people of different fitness levels. They are also all the same gender – should sample people of both genders.

Idea 3: all the same age range – should sample people of different ages.

b There isn't a time period given. 'Sport' isn't defined: does walking the dog (which is exercise) count, or does it have to be competitive?

c There is no box for less than 1 hour. The others overlap – if you do exactly 2 hours' sport, for example, you can choose either the first or the second box.

9

a $(x - 6) \times (x - 1)$

$= x^2 - 7x + 6$

So Vanessa is correct

Area involves multiplying, so it is likely that x^2 will be involved, so Vanessa's expression looks more plausible. To work out the area of a rectangle we do length × width.

b $4x - 14 = 2(2x - 7)$

Perimeter is the distance around the outside of the shape.

Perimeter $= 4x - 14$

This can be factorised to give $2(2x - 7)$, which is Doug's expression.

10 $\sqrt{81} = 9$

Start by working out each one.

$4^2 - 2^3 = 16 - 8 = 8$

$\sqrt[3]{1000} = 10$

$\sqrt[5]{25} \div 9^0 = 5 \times 5 \div 1 = 25 \div 1 = 25$

$3^{-2} \times 3^2 = 1 \div 9 \times 9 = 1$

$(\sqrt{36})^2 = 6^2 = 36$

1, 8, 9, 10, 25, 36

Now put the values in order, from smallest to largest.

$3^{-2} \times 3^2, 4^2 - 2^3, \sqrt{81}, \sqrt[3]{1000}, 5\sqrt{25} \div 9^0, (\sqrt{36})^2$

Finally write the numbers in order in their original formats.

a 1048 km/h

$655 \div 5 \times 8$

b 1 hour 40 minutes

Distance ÷ speed = 1746 ÷ 1048 = 1.66 hours = 1 hour 40 minutes

c 9 hours 15 minutes

$9700 \div 1048 = 9\frac{1}{4}$ hours

d Take-off, accelerating up to speed, decelerating and landing are all at much lower speeds. There might also be strong winds and bad weather.

12 **a** 1500 m ÷ 200 m = 7.5

Given that the other track is twice as long, he will need half as many laps.

Simon will need to run 7.5 laps of the indoor running track and 3.75 laps (i.e. 1500 / 400) of the outdoor running track to cover 1500 m.

b 5 km = 5000 m

5000 m ÷ 200 m = 25

Denise will have to run 25 laps of the indoor track and 12.5 laps of the outdoor track to cover 5 km.

The 10 km is double the 5 km race, so Denise will have to run 50 laps of the indoor track and 25 laps of the outdoor track to cover 10 km.

13 **a** $T = 40k + 25$

$40k + 25$, where k is the number of kilograms.

b Uncle Bertie is wrong; the lamb doesn't need to go into the oven until 9.25 am

$40 \times 3.75 + 25$ plus an extra 10 minutes of time is 185 minutes. This is the same as 3 hours and 5 minutes.

 a

This is one way to list all the possibilities in a systematic way.

		Day 1		
		Swim	**Jog**	**Cycle**
Day 2	**Swim**	SS	JS	CS
	Jog	SJ	JJ	CJ
	Cycle	SC	JC	CC

b $\frac{1}{9}$

c $\frac{6}{9} = \frac{2}{3}$ All of the combinations except SS, JJ and CC.

This is sensible because whichever one is chosen for Day 1, there are 2 out of the 3 that can be chosen on Day 2.

15 A pie chart tells you about proportions, not about numbers. The question tells you that all the Year 8 students are there, but only a few from Year 9, so even though a large fraction of Year 9 students want to swim, this may not be many people.

You can approach this by thinking about what is sensible.

16 The pie chart shows the proportion of the boys' pets that are dogs, cats etc. We don't know whether one boy owns all the rabbits, for example, or whether there are the same number of boys as there are girls.

This means that we cannot draw any conclusions from the pie charts.

You can deal with this by thinking about exactly what information the pie chart is giving you, and what it isn't giving you.

17

a Coach Cooksey will have the more accurate mean height as he is using the actual height of each of his members. Coach McKay is finding the estimated mean using the midpoints of each class width. By using the midpoints he is giving each member in each class interval the same height.

Team McKay			
Height (cm)	**Midpoint**	**Frequency**	**Midpoint × frequency**
$145 \leqslant h < 155$	150	1	150
$155 \leqslant h < 165$	160	2	320
$165 \leqslant h < 175$	170	2	340
$175 \leqslant h < 185$	180	8	1440
$185 \leqslant h < 195$	190	3	570
$195 \leqslant h < 225$	210	4	840
	Totals:	20	3660

$3660 \div 20 = 183$

b 183 cm

c The mean height is the same for both teams at 183 cm. But Team Cooksey has both the shortest member (= height 142 cm) and the tallest member (= height 226 cm), so a larger range of heights.

18   **a**   Glass 1 contains $\frac{1}{4}$ units of squash.

Glass 2 contains $\frac{1}{6}$ units of squash.

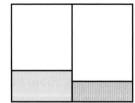

With questions like this it can help to assign a volume to the glass, be it a numerical value or an algebraic one.

Assume the volume of each glass is 1 unit so that you can just work with the fraction in the question.

Pouring the two glasses together results in a total volume of 2 units.

The squash from glass 1 now represents $\frac{1}{8}$ of the combined drink.

The squash from glass 2 now represents $\frac{1}{12}$ of the combined drink.

$$\frac{1}{8} + \frac{1}{12} = \frac{3}{24} + \frac{2}{24} = \frac{5}{24}$$

So the resulting drink is $\frac{5}{24}$ squash.

Notice that this will produce a drink that is weaker than glass 1 and stronger than glass 2.

b   The strength of the final drink will be between the two strengths of the original drinks. $\frac{2}{5}$ and $\frac{3}{10}$ are both less than $\frac{1}{2}$ so it is not possible to make a drink that is exactly $\frac{1}{2}$ apple.

---

19   **a**   10% of 90 g = 9 g

5% of 90 g = $\frac{9\,g}{2}$ = 4.5 g

The low fat yoghurt contains more sugar per pot (5.9 g compared to 4.5 g for the 'full fat' version).

b $\frac{5.9\,g}{104\,g}$ = 0.056730…

0.56730… × 100% = 5.6730…%

$\frac{4.5\,g}{90\,g}$ = 5%

The low fat yoghurt contains approximately 5.7% of the GDA of sugar.

The full fat yoghurt contains 5% of the GDA of sugar.

Calculate the amount of sugar in grams in the second yoghurt.

Conclusion

First consider the low fat yoghurt.

Next consider the full fat yoghurt.

Conclusion

20 a

Planet	Distance from Sun in AU	Shortest distance to next orbit in AU
Mercury	0.387	0.336
Venus	0.723	0.277
Earth	1	0.524
Mars	1.524	3.679
Jupiter	5.203	4.32
Saturn	9.523	9.685
Uranus	19.208	10.879
Neptune	30.087	–

The distance between the orbits of Venus and Earth is 0.277 AU.

b $0.277 \times 9.3 \times 10^7 = 25\,761\,000$ miles
(or 2.5761×10^7 miles)

Earth is never closer than 25 million miles to Venus.

The planets are not always the same distance apart. If Earth and Mars are on the same side of the Sun then they will be closer than if they are on opposite sides. That is why the question asks for the 'shortest possible distance'.

21

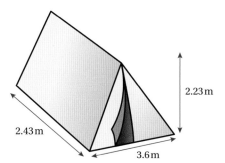

2.23 m

2.43 m

3.6 m

Peter is 2.03 m tall so the tent needs to be at least this long. You might assume that to be comfortable Peter will need the tent to be a little longer, for example an extra 20 cm at his head and at his feet.

To decide how wide the tent needs to be you have to make an assumption about the 'width' of Peter and his three friends. You want it to be comfortable so you should be generous with your estimate. Perhaps allowing 90 cm per person is reasonable.

Peter also needs to be able to stand up in the tent. If the tent is 2.03 m tall then Peter would just about be able to stand up in the middle (but his head would touch the top). So again, make it more comfortable and given him a little extra room, say 20 cm.

1 **a** 37 runs

b It depends. Here is a table showing the number of runs Ben might score and the number that John would get:

Ben	0	1	2	3	4	5	6	7	8	9	10	11	12	13
John	–14	–11	–8	–5	–2	1	4	7	10	13	16	19	22	25

After this, John's score will increase faster than Ben's.

If Ben usually scores less than 7 then he is better, but if he usually scores more than 7 then John is better.

c If Ben scores 4 runs or fewer then John would have a negative number of runs, which is not possible.

2 $\frac{1}{3}$ of 12 = 4 purple sections

$\frac{1}{6}$ of 12 = 2 red sections

$\frac{1}{12}$ of 12 = 1 green section

4 + 2 + 1 = 7

12 – 7 = 5 blue sections

You could draw a diagram of the spinner and colour it in.

3 **i** and **ii** The only numbers on the dice are 1, 2, 3 and 4.

iii There is only one 1.

iv Six of the numbers are 2 or 4.

v Three of the numbers are 1 or 4.

Each piece of information tells you something useful.

iii tells you there is one 1, and **v** tells you there are two 4s. **iv** then means there are four 2s, so the other number must be a 3.

The numbers are: 1, 2, 2, 2, 2, 3, 4, 4

Five of these are prime numbers, so the probability of getting a prime is $\frac{5}{8}$.

4 **a** $\frac{1}{6}$

b $\frac{1}{6} \times 12 = 2$

While it is possible that zero sixes or 12 sixes are rolled, the expected number of sixes is two. **However**, this is the expected average number over many sets of 12 throws, so Bashir is not completely correct.

probability of an event × total number of outcomes = expected number of favourable outcomes

5 **a**

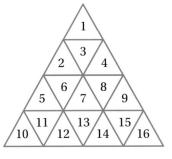

There are 16 small triangles.

All equilateral triangles are similar because they all have three equal angles (of 60°).

b 1, 2, 3, 4

2, 5, 6, 7

4, 7, 8, 9

5, 10, 11, 12

7, 12, 13, 14

9, 14, 15, 16

6, 7, 8, 13

So there are 7 equilateral triangles of this size.

1, 2, 3, 4, 5, 6, 7, 8, 9

2, 5, 6, 7, 10, 11, 12, 13, 14

4, 7, 8, 9, 12, 13, 14, 15, 16

So there are 3 equilateral triangles of this size.

16 small + 7 medium + 3 large + 1 extra large = 27 similar triangles

Triangles 1, 2, 3 and 4 make another equilateral triangle. Count all the equilateral triangles of this size.

Triangles 1, 2, 3, 4, 5, 6, 7, 8 and 9 make a larger equilateral triangle. Count all of these.

Finally there is a single extra large equilateral triangle made from all 16 smaller triangles.

6 **a**

This is likely to be a triangular prism

A sketch might help:

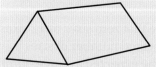

b

A sketch suggests a pyramid.

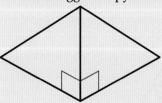

c

A sketch suggests another triangular prism.

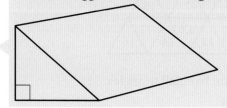

7 Candice should give the mean length.

The mode = 11 cm

The median = 10.25 cm

The mean = 9.833 cm

8 **a**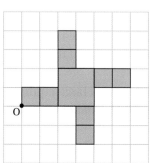

b 0 lines of symmetry

c rotational symmetry order 4

d 1 Draw a circle of radius 1 cm.

   2 Enlarge this circle by a scale factor of 2 about the centre of the circle.

   3 Translate the small circle 2 cm to the left.

   4 Translate the small central circle 2 cm to the right.

There are several ways this image could be created. Here is one possible set of instructions.

9 **a** Jillian's polygon is a regular pentagon.

It has 5 sides. 5 is a prime number.

It has rotational symmetry of order 5.

All the interior angles are obtuse (greater than 90° but less than 180°).

b *I am a quadrilateral.* This describes any four-sided shape.

I have two pairs of parallel sides. The following quadrilaterals match this description: square, rectangle, parallelogram, rhombus.

c To get the answer 'rectangle', she could add: 'the angles are all equal but my sides are not'

To get the answer 'rhombus' she could add: 'the sides are all equal but my angles are not'

To get the answer 'square', she could add: 'the angles are all 90° and the sides are all the same length'

All of them are already parallelograms, so she doesn't need to add anything.

10 Shape **A**, the circle, could be the circular face of the cylinder (the cross-sectional area), the base of a cone or any view of a sphere.

Shape **B**, the square, could be any face of a cube, a square face of a cuboid or the curved surface of a cylinder.

All three boys were correct.

To answer this question, you need to take each of the boys' answers in turn and decide whether one of the faces of their 3-D shapes matches the plan views.

11

a $\frac{2}{3}$ as a decimal is 0.666... so $\frac{2}{3}$ > 0.66.

b $0.25 = \frac{1}{4}$

$\frac{8}{32} = \frac{1}{4}$, so $0.25 = \frac{8}{32}$

c $\frac{3}{11} = 0.272\,727...$

so $\frac{3}{11}$ < 0.273

> It is much easier to compare them if they are both fractions or are both decimals.

> In this pair, the fraction can actually be simplified. This will make the comparison easier.

> Use short division to evaluate the decimal equivalent to $\frac{3}{11}$.

> In this question it is easier to compare the decimals (finding a common denominator to compare the fractions is not as easy).

d $0.05 = \frac{5}{100} = \frac{1}{20}$,

$\frac{1}{20} > \frac{1}{22}$, so $0.05 > \frac{1}{22}$

e Here is a diagram showing 0.49.

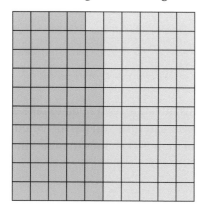

Now if you shade 0.499 9 of the shape you get this (there is a tiny part of that top square which hasn't been shaded):

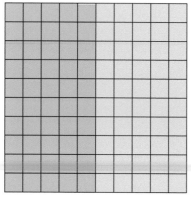

If you keep on doing this you get closer and closer to 0.5 each time, so you say that 0.4999 ... = 0.5

a 9 cm²

b One way to split Y is:

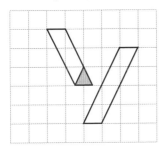

Area of right-hand parallelogram = 1 cm × 4 cm = 4 cm²

Area of left-hand piece = (1 cm × 3 cm) – (0.5 × 1 cm × 1 cm) = 3 cm² – 0.5 cm² = 2.5 cm²

4 cm² + 2.5 cm² = 6.5 cm²

c The letters B and D both fit inside a rectangle of area 12 cm².

To make the B you need to subtract 1 square. To make the D you need to subtract more than 1 square, so the B has a bigger area.

d The smallest area will be the letter I.

The area of the letter H can be found very easily by counting squares.

The letter Y can be split into the shapes shown in the diagram.

An alternative is to assemble parts to make whole squares.

Area of a parallelogram = base × perpendicular height

Area of left hand piece = area of parallelogram – area of shaded triangle

Total area of Y.

Area of a parallelogram = base × perpendicular height

13

You could draw a few more diagrams and could then make a table of results to see whether that will help you understand what is going on (although it won't explain it).

Pattern number	1	2	3	4
Number of metal rods	6	12	18	24
Number of wooden rods	7	12	17	22

a 18

The number of metal rods goes up by 6 each time because each new panel has 6 metal rods in it.

b 22

The number of wooden rods goes up by 5 each time because when a new panel is added, the left-hand side is joined to the previous panel.

c $6n$

d The $6 \times 12 = 72$ metal rods will cost £144, and the $5 \times 12 + 2 = 62$ wooden rods will cost £155.

The total cost is £299.

14 **a**

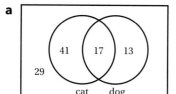

A Venn diagram will help to show what is going on.

Fill in the 17 first.

Then use the information about how many people own a dog.

Then use the information about how many people own either a dog or a cat but not both.

Finally, fill in the ones who own neither a dog nor a cat.

b $\dfrac{29}{100}$

c $\dfrac{41}{100}$

15 **a** Equilateral triangle

You know that the angles in an equilateral triangle are all 60°.

b i Square

You know that all the angles in a square are 90°.

ii Regular hexagon

The exterior angle = 180° – 120° = 60°

The sum of exterior angles is 360° for all polygons.

360° ÷ n = 60° (where n is the number of sides of the polygon).

$n = 6$

iii Regular decagon

Similarly to shape **ii**, the exterior angle is 180° – 144° = 36°

360° ÷ 36° gives 10 sides.

16 **a**

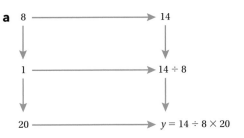

Work out the scale factor for the larger triangle

$y = 35$ cm

b Triangle ABC has area 80 cm².

Triangle XYZ has area 245 cm².

c The ratio is 80 : 245, which simplifies to 16 : 49.

d 16 and 49 are both square numbers.

The ratio of the sides is 4 : 7.

The ratio of the areas is $4^2 : 7^2$.

17 $a^2 + b^2 = c^2$

$2.1^2 + 1.05^2 = c^2$

$5.5125 = c^2$

$c = \sqrt{5.5125} = 2.347\ldots\,\mathrm{m}$

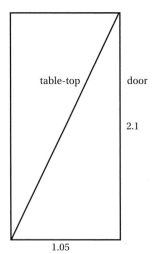

Arthur's new table has a diameter of 240 cm. Even if Arthur turns the table to try to go through the door diagonally, it will not fit. It is more than 5 cm too big.

2.4 metres is more than the height of the door. Even when it is tilted it will be a close-run thing as to whether it will fit.

18

a The blue graph is MoveIt Builders. The red graphs is JCE.

b MoveIt Builders = £15

c £14

d Less, Daily charge £12, £2 per day

e £75

f £183

g MoveIt Builders

h £13 cheaper

£70 for 5 days, daily rate = £70 ÷ 5

MoveIt Builders 75 for 5 days (75 − 15 = 60, 60 ÷ 5)

15 + (12 × 14)

14 × 14 = 196

19

Write the lengths as ordinary numbers.

a Rectangle **B** has the bigger perimeter.

Perimeter of **A** is $16 + 9 + 16 + 9 = 50$

Perimeter of **B** is $25 + 2 + 25 + 2 = 54$

b Rectangle **A** has the bigger area.

Area of **A** is $16 \times 9 = 144$

Area of **B** is $25 \times 2 = 50$

20 **a** $1\,m^3 = 1\,m \times 1\,m \times 1\,m$

$1\,m^3 = 100\,cm \times 100\,cm \times 100\,cm$

$1\,m^3 = 1\,000\,000\,cm^3$

So Anna was incorrect to think that she should multiply by 100.

Alternatively, you could spot that Anna is wrong by thinking about how small $15\,cm^3$ is. $15\,cm^3$ is the volume of a cuboid that is $1\,cm \times 1\,cm \times 15\,cm$ (the height of your ruler).

This wouldn't be very much water to have a bath in!

b $0.15 \times 1\,000\,000 = 150\,000\,cm^3$

c $150\,000\,ml \div 1000 = 150$ litres $(1\,cm^3 = 1\,ml)$

21 **a**

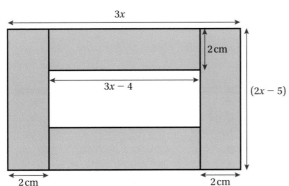

This is one way to split up the shape.

The top rectangle has area: $2(3x - 4) = 6x - 8$

The left rectangle has area: $2(2x - 5) = 4x - 10$

Altogether all four rectangles add up to $20x - 36$

b $20x - 36 = 204$

$20x = 240$

$x = 12$

This means $3x$ is 36 and $(2x - 5)$ is 19.

The dimensions are $36\,cm$ by $19\,cm$.

a $4x + 5y = 205$ (equation 1)

$3x + 7y = 235$ (equation 2)

Let x be the price of each apple in pence, and y be the price of each banana in pence.

b and **c**

One way to solve this is to get the same number of xs in each equation.

$12x + 28y = 940$

Multiply equation 2 through by 4

$12x + 15y = 615$

Multiply equation 1 through by 3

$13y = 325$

Subtract

$y = 25$

Divide by 13

This means a banana costs 25 pence.

$4x + 5 \times 25 = 205$

Substitute $y = 35$ into equation 1.

$4x = 80$

$x = 20$ so an apple costs 20 pence.

---

 a 80% of £10 is £1 × 8 = £8. 75% of £12 is $\frac{3}{4}$ of £12 = £9. 75% of £12 is more money.

b One way is to work out that 20% of one hour is 12 minutes, whereas $\frac{3}{8}$ of half an hour is $11\frac{1}{4}$ minutes. An alternative is to compare 20% with $\frac{3}{8}$ of a half. $\frac{3}{8} \times \frac{1}{2} = \frac{3}{16}$ but 20% $= \frac{1}{5} = \frac{3}{15}$, so 20% is bigger

c 50% of 1 is a half. 25% of 2 is also $\frac{1}{2}$. They are the same.

d We don't need to do any difficult calculations. A 10% discount would be £1.30, which is less than the £1.99 postage charge, so a 5% discount is not enough and it would be cheaper to buy it in the shop.

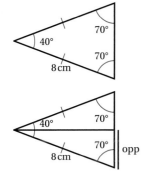

You can use the fact that triangle **A** is isosceles to work out the other angles.

Splitting an isosceles triangle in half gives two right-angled triangles, so in triangle **A**:

Opp = $8 \times sin20° = 2.73616...$ cm

The length of the third side is twice this length.

$2 \times 2.73616... = 5.4723...$ cm

Triangle **B** is isosceles and is congruent to triangle **A**.

Triangle **C** doesn't have any lengths marked on it, so while it is similar to **A** and **B** you don't know that it is congruent.

Triangle **D** is not congruent to the others because the third side is 5.5 cm instead of 5.4723... cm

A and **B** are definitely congruent, so statement **e** is correct.

a There are two possibilities:

Rotate A 180° about (0,3)

Enlarge A by a scale factor of –1 about point (0,3)

b There are a lot of possibilities:

Do two reflections (e.g. in the line $x = 0$ and then in the line $y = 3$).

Do a rotation and a translation (e.g. rotate A 180° about (–2,3) and then translate it 4 units to the right

Do a translation and then a rotation, or two enlargements, or an enlargement and a translation.

1 **a**

+	1	2	3	4	5	6	7	8	9
1									
2									
3									
4									
5									
6									
7									
8									
9									

Pair up every integer with every other integer systematically.

The table illustrates all the possible calculations that can be made.

Notice that these are different calculations. They do not necessarily represent different answers.

If you want to assume that 2 + 5 is a different calculation from 5 + 2 then you need all 81 cells, otherwise you only need the shaded ones.

b

	-9	-8	-7	-6	-5	-4	-3	-2	-1
-9	-18	-17	-16	-15	-14	-13	-12	-11	-10
-8	-17	-16	-15	-14	-13	-12	-11	-10	-9
-7	-16	-15	-14	-13	-12	-11	-10	-9	-8
-6	-15	-14	-13	-12	-11	-10	-9	-8	-7
-5	-14	-13	-12	-11	-10	-9	-8	-7	-6
-4	-13	-12	-11	-10	-9	-8	-7	-6	-5
-3	-12	-11	-10	-9	-8	-7	-6	-5	-4
-2	-11	-10	-9	-8	-7	-6	-5	-4	-3
-1	-10	-9	-8	-7	-6	-5	-4	-3	-2

The purple cells show the 17 different answers you can get.

2

1 can't do

2 can't do

3 can't do

4 can't do

5 can't do

6 = 3 + 3

7 can't do

8 = 3 + 5

9 = 3 + 3 + 3

10 = 5 + 5

11 = 3 + 5 + 3

12 = 3 + 3 + 3 + 3

7 is the largest number you cannot make.

This is an obvious one to work through systematically, but how will you know when to stop?

Now you might notice that you can make 11 by adding 3 onto the way you made 8. To make 12 you can add 3 onto 9, to make 13 you can add 3 onto 10. This means you can always make every number bigger than 7 by adding on extra 3s.

7 is the lowest number you cannot make.

3

1 only has 1 factor	7 prime	13 prime
2 prime	8 factors are 1, 2, 4, 8	14 factors are 1, 2, 7, 14
3 prime	9 factors are 1, 3, 9	15 factors are 1, 3, 5, 15
4 factors are 1, 2, 4	10 factors are 1, 2, 5, 10	16 factors are 1, 2, 4, 8, 16
5 prime	11 prime	17 prime
6 factors are 1, 2, 3, 6	12 factors are 1, 2, 3, 4, 6, 12	(needs to be smaller than 18)

You could work through this systematically, working out the number of factors that each number has got. You can save yourself some time by recalling that prime numbers have exactly two factors, so you can eliminate them immediately.

Number 12 has the most factors.

4   **a** $16 \times 130\,\text{mm} = 2080\,\text{mm} = 208\,\text{cm}$

> 16 edges of hexagons make up the perimeter.

      b The perimeter is 156 cm and each side is 13 cm

          $156 \div 13\,\text{cm} = 12$ tiles

> 12 edges need to be 'exposed'.
>
> You could try 2 hexagons and see that this won't give you enough sides (there are only 10), and then try 3 hexagons in a line and find there are 14 sides, so there must be a different collection of 3 hexagons that will work.

      This can be done with three interlocking hexagons, each showing four edges.

---

 5   **a**

Number of flowers	1	2	3
Number of blue beads	6	12	18

      18 blue beads are needed

      b Each flower needs 6 blue beads so the nth term is $6n$.

---

 6   **a** 30

> We are using relative frequency, so if you double the throws, you need to double the number of sixes.

      b $7 \times 50 = 350$

> 105 sixes are seven times as many as 15 sixes, so you need seven times as many throws.

      c $0.3 \times 1200 = 360$

> Part **a** tells you the relative frequency is $\dfrac{30}{100} = 0.3$

---

 7 $98 + 105 + 110 + 108 + 99 = 520$

> Find the total number of students.

     $\dfrac{110}{520} = \dfrac{11}{52}$

> There are 110 students in Year 9.

8 **a** $10 \times 7 = 70$
$11 \times 6 = 66$
$10 \times 7 > 11 \times 6$

You could work out answers to all the multiplications and compare them, but there are quicker ways for some of them.

b $-44 \times 5 = 44 \times -5$

You don't need to work out that both of them equal –220. They contain the same numbers and one of them is positive and one is negative each time. This means that the answers are the same.

c $972\,310 \times 0 < 1 \times 1$

While it is easy to work out the answers to this one you don't need to, because you know that anything multiplied by zero is zero, and the second answer is positive.

d $91 \times -2 < 59 \times 3$

The first answer is negative (because there is a positive number multiplied by a negative number), whereas the second answer is positive (because there are two positive numbers multiplied together). This means you don't need to work out the exact answers (–182 and 117).

9 **i** $100 \div (5^2 \times 2)$
$100 \div (25 \times 2)$
$100 \div 50 = 2$

The only sensible way to answer this question seems to be to work out each answer. Remember the correct order of operations (where, for example, brackets are worked out first).

ii $620 \times 4 \div 248$
$2480 \div 248 = 10$

iii $81 - 37 \times 2$
$81 - 74 = 7$

Using the correct order of operations, multiplication comes before subtraction. 37×2 must be done first.

iv $-27 \div -3 + 12$
$9 + 12 = 21$
Calculation **i** is the smallest.

10 $+ - \times$ $5 + 2 - 10 \times 3 = 5 + 2 - -30 = 5 + 2 + 30 = 37$

Make a systematic list of the arrangements of the three operations and then calculate the answers.

$+ \times -$ $5 + 2 \times 10 - -3 = 5 + 20 + 3 = 28$
$- + \times$ $5 - 2 + 10 \times -3 = 5 - 2 - 30 = -27$
$- \times +$ $5 - 2 \times 10 + -3 = 5 - 20 - 3 = -18$
$\times + -$ $5 \times 2 + 10 - -3 = 10 + 10 + 3 = 23$
$\times - +$ $5 \times 2 - 10 + -3 = 10 - 10 - 3 = -3$

You can achieve a negative result in three different ways.

11 **a i**

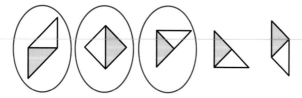

With two sandwiches it is possible to create three polygons: a right-angled isosceles triangle, a parallelogram and a square.

If you have two sandwiches (two triangles) then it might make sense to keep one of them fixed and move the other around it. Here the blue one is fixed and the white one moves.

There are three different positions in which the second sandwich could be placed.

ii

If you have three sandwiches (three triangles) then it makes sense to start with the three arrangements for two sandwiches and move the third sandwich around these.

The second and third ones are congruent to the first one – and the others that start with a square will also all be congruent.

The third one is congruent to the ones above. All the others that start with the parallelogram will be congruent to others that we have already got.

This is the only new one.

With three sandwiches it is possible to create four polygons: two different trapeziums and two different irregular pentagons.

Conclusion

iii

If you have four sandwiches (four triangles) then it makes sense to start with the four arrangements for three sandwiches and move the fourth sandwich around these.

Again, some of these are identical or are reflections of each other.

These are the ones that are distinct.

With four sandwiches it is possible to create nine polygons: a rectangle, four different irregular hexagons, an isosceles trapezium, a parallelogram, an isosceles triangle and a square.

b   Yes.

This is almost a trick question. A square is an example of all the special quadrilaterals (it is also a rectangle, a parallelogram, a rhombus, a kite and a trapezium), so the original sandwich works for all of them.

12 **a i** $2 \times 3 \times 4 = 24$

Gemma appears to be multiplying the numbers.

    ii Gemma is not correct, as 12 is the smallest integer that is divisible by 2, 3 and 4

24 is divisible by 2, 3 and 4.

    iii Lidia's method:

Lidia's method is to work systematically checking each number.

This will get her the correct answer. However, it takes a long time.

It can't be smaller than 6 because those numbers didn't work for both 2 and 3.

It can't be 6 because 4 won't work.

It can't be 7 because none of the numbers will work.

It can't be 8 because 3 won't work.

It can't be 9 because 2 and 4 won't work.

It can't be 10 because 3 and 4 won't work.

It can't be 11 because none of the numbers work.

It can be 12 because 12 is divisible by 2, 3 and 4. The answer is 12.

Harry's method:

Harry's method is to write out the times tables and look for common multiples.

His method is good: it gets him the correct answer and is quicker than Lidia's method in this case.

However, if the question was about different numbers that have times tables that aren't as quick to write down, or that don't have common multiples very early on in the lists, Harry's method would take much longer.

2, 4, 6, 8, 10, 12, 14, 16, 18, 20, ...

3, 6, 9, 12, 15, 18, 21, 24, 27, ...

4, 8, 12, ...

12 is in all three lists. The answer is 12.

    iv You are trying to work out the Lowest Common Multiple of 2, 3 and 4.

$2 \times 2 \times 3$ will do this, giving an answer of 12.

  b 30 is the smallest number exactly divisible by 3, 5 and 6.

Whichever method you use you should get 30 as the answer.

13 **a** Box 1: four cylinders of radius 10 cm and height 15 cm

Box 2: one cylinder of radius 20 cm and height 15 cm

Box 3: sixteen cylinders of radius 5 cm and height 15 cm

b Students' guesses

c Box 1: volume of cylinders $= \pi \times 10^2 \times 15 \times 4 = 6000\pi$

Box 2: volume of cylinders $= \pi \times 20^2 \times 15 = 6000\pi$

Box 3: volume of cylinders $= \pi \times 5^2 \times 15 \times 16 = 6000\pi$

Because the total volume of the cylinders is the same each time the unused space is the same in each box.

Did this answer surprise you? Or did you guess that all three boxes had the same amount of unused space?

If you look at each calculation for the volume of the cylinders, you will notice that each has $\pi \times 15$. The rest of the calculation for each volume multiplies to give the same answer, 400.

$4 \times 10^2 = 20^2 = 16 \times 5^2 = 400$

 14 **a**

	crisps	fruit	yoghurt
water	sandwich, crisps, water	sandwich, fruit, water	sandwich, yoghurt, water
juice	sandwich, crisps, juice	sandwich, fruit, juice	sandwich, yoghurt, juice

Every meal includes a sandwich, so you only need to consider crisps/fruit/yoghurt and water/juice. A table is a good way to show this.

b $\frac{2}{6} = \frac{1}{3}$

two combinations out of six that include yoghurt

c $\frac{2}{6} \times 330 = 110$

two combinations out of six that include crisps

 15

Be careful: the question says the number is greater than 1 and less than 50 so it can only be from 2 to 49.

a $\frac{24}{48} = \frac{1}{2}$

There are 48 numbers and 24 of them are even.

b $\frac{1}{2}$

All the other numbers are odd.

c $\frac{9}{48} = \frac{3}{16}$

There are 9 multiples of 5.

d $\frac{1}{48}$

e $\frac{9}{48} = \frac{3}{16}$

The factors of 48 that are between 1 and 50 are: 2, 3, 4, 6, 8, 12, 16, 24 and 48.

16 $12 \times 50\,\text{p} = £6$ (12 coins)

$9 \times £1 = £9$ (9 coins)

$£47 - £6 - £9 = £32$, which is 16 £2 coins

$12 + 9 + 16 = 37$ coins in total

$\dfrac{16}{37}$

> First work out how many £2 coins there are.

---

17 a

	Circle	Star	Triangle
Heart	CH	SH	TH
Rabbit	CR	SR	TR
Car	CC	SC	TC

> This is one way to list all the possibilities in a systematic way.

b $\dfrac{1}{9}$

---

18 a $\dfrac{3}{12} = \dfrac{1}{4}$

> 3 blues and 12 pens in total

b $\dfrac{3}{12} \times \dfrac{2}{11} = \dfrac{6}{132}$

> If the first pen was blue, two blue pens are left out of the remaining 11 pens.
>
> Multiply the probability of the two independent events.

$\dfrac{1}{22}$

> simplify

19 **a** 12 panels ÷ 4 = 3 panels on each side

$3 \times 60\,\text{cm} = 180\,\text{cm}$

A diagram will help with this question.

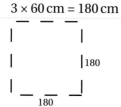

The area is $180\,\text{cm} \times 180\,\text{cm} = 32\,400\,\text{cm}^2$

b

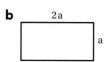

Let the number of panels along the shorter side be a.

From the number of panels available:

$12 = 2a + a + 2a + a = 6a$

$a = 12 \div 6 = 2$

The run is 4 panels long and 2 panels wide.

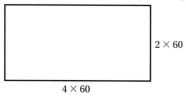

This area is $240\,\text{cm} \times 120\,\text{cm} = 28\,800\,\text{cm}^2$

Adam is not correct. The rectangular pen has a smaller area than the square pen.

c 12 panels ÷ 3 = 4 panels per side.

$4 \times 60\,\text{cm} = 240\,\text{cm}$

Area of a triangle = $0.5 \times$ base $\times$ height (h)

Use Pythagoras' theorem to work out the height of the triangle.

$h^2 = 240^2 - 120^2$

$h^2 = 43\,200$

$h = 206.846\ldots\,\text{cm}$

Area $= \frac{1}{2} \times 240\,\text{cm} \times 207.846\ldots\,\text{cm}$

$= 24\,941.53\ldots\,\text{cm}^2$, which is smaller than the square one, so Kim is wrong.

20

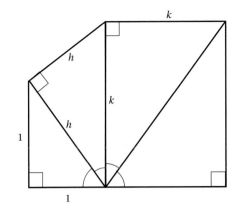

This problem can be solved using some of the strategies from earlier chapters. First label the diagram. You could also put it on the things you know.

a All the triangles are similar, so they must all be isosceles.

$1^2 + 1^2 + = h^2$

$2 = h^2$

$h^2 + h^2 = k^2$

$2 + 2 = k^2$

$k = 2$

The fourth triangle is the same as the third one, so the width is 2 and the height is 2.

The area of the first triangle is $\frac{1}{2}$ and the area of the largest one is 2, so the area has been multiplied by 4.

b The triangles are all isosceles and have a right angle, so the other two angles must be 45° each. The four angles that are marked are all 45°, which adds up to 180° so it does form a straight line.

Focus on the first triangle on the left and use Pythagoras' theorem.

In the next triangle

You know that all powers of 1 are 1, so this means that $2^b + 3^c = 244$.

This question can be worked out in several systematic ways. Here is one.

You don't need to worry about negative powers of 2 and 3 because they will give fractions.

You could make a list of powers of 2 and powers of 3, but consider for a moment that 3^c is always odd. The only way to get an even result (like 244) is for 2^b to be odd.

So this must be $2^0 = 1$ and $3^c = 243$

The only way 2^b can be an odd number is if $b = 0$

3^0	1
3^1	3
3^2	9
3^3	27
3^4	81
3^5	243

This means that:

a can be anything

$b = 0$

$c = 5$

1

a In Dallas, each room costs $75 for one person plus $35 per extra person and each room has three beds.

In one room, it will cost $75 for the first person, $35 for the second person and $35 for the third person. That makes $145 in total for each room for three people.

There are 15 people altogether, so they need five rooms and overall this will cost:

$145 × 5 = $725

There is a lot of information given in the question. Pick out the pieces that you need to solve the answer.

b In Las Vegas, the motel has rooms with four beds, so they will need three full rooms and one with three people in it.

A diagram might help.

Room 1: ($75) ($35) ($35) ($35)   4 people, cost = $180

Room 2: ($75) ($35) ($35) ($35)   4 people, cost = $180

Room 3: ($75) ($35) ($35) ($35)   4 people, cost = $180

Room 4: ($75) ($35) ($35)   4 people, cost = $145

Total cost is $685.

$725 – $685 = $40

It is $40 cheaper to stay in Las Vegas.

c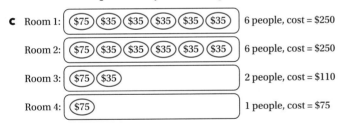

Room 1: ($75) ($35) ($35) ($35) ($35) ($35)   6 people, cost = $250

Room 2: ($75) ($35) ($35) ($35) ($35) ($35)   6 people, cost = $250

Room 3: ($75) ($35)   2 people, cost = $110

Room 4: ($75)   1 people, cost = $75

The question doesn't tell you to work out how much it will cost in San Francisco, but you will need to if you want to know which city is cheapest.

The total cost is $685, so Las Vegas and San Francisco are equally cheapest at $685.

2 There are 12 inches in 1 foot, so 5 feet 10 inches is:

$5 \times 12 + 10 = 70$ inches

> You know that Sarah is 5 feet 10 inches tall and that 1 inch is approximately 2.5 cm. Maybe the best thing to start with is to convert her height into inches.

70 inches = 70×2.5 cm = 175 cm

This means that Leon is 5 cm taller than Sarah, so he is correct.

---

3 He will have $3 left.

$3 ÷ 1.70 = £1.76

> There are two ways to do this. Here is one:

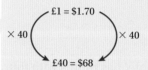

---

4 **a**

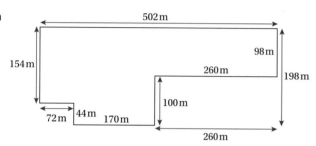

> Use the diagram in the question but try to complete the missing labels.

The total length is 1400 m. Three laps will be:

1400 m × 3 = 4200 m, which is 4.2 km

> Once all the sides are labelled, you could add them all up to find the length of one lap.
>
> Alternatively, you could use the fact that the length of the track is the same as the perimeter of the rectangle that has been drawn around the edge.

b The runners have run 7 laps in total.

1400 m × 7 = 9800 m, which is 9.8 km

---

5 **a** Jyoti's tower = $1 + 2 + 3 + 4 + 5 + 6 = 21$ cm

Laura's tower = $7 + 8 + 9 + 10 + 11 + 12 = 57$ cm

Laura's tower is 36 cm taller.

> The total height of all the cubes is 78 cm.
>
> $78 ÷ 2 = 39$ cm gives the height when they are the same.

b $57 + 21 = 78$ cm

One possible answer is $1 + 2 + 3 + 10 + 11 + 12 = 39$
and $4 + 5 + 6 + 7 + 8 + 9 = 39$

> Each girl must now have a combination that is 39 cm high.

6

i   True

> If you add the digits of the number together you get 48, which is divisible by 3, so the number is also divisible by 3.

ii   False

> The number is a multiple of 3, so it cannot be prime. It is also even.

iii   True

> The number 12 345 678 910 is in the 5 times table, so if you divide 12 345 678 912 by 5 then the remainder is 2.

iv   True

> The last two digits are 12, which is a multiple of 4, so the number is a multiple of 4. Tip: if a number is a multiple of 4 then the last two digits will be also be a multiple of 4.

7   Grandad's age is $2x$, Geoff's age is x and Paul's age is $x - 28$.

> One way to do this is to call Geoff's age x and to work out the other ages in terms of x.

In total this is $2x + x + x - 28$, which equals 112.

$4x - 28 = 112$, so $4x = 140$ and $x = 35$.

Grandad Jones is 70 years old, Geoff is 35 years old and Paul is 7 years old.

8   **a** $c = 17 \times 55 + 60$

$c = 995$

£9.95

b $2100 = 17n + 60$

$n = 120$

c   A 55-word advert costs £9.95 and the formula tells you that if you increase the number of words by 1 then the cost will increase by 17 pence. This means that 55 words is the most Jolene can get for £10.

> You know the answer to part **c** already, because part **a** has given it away.

9 $\pi \times 4^2 \times 15 = 753.98 \, \text{cm}^3$ (2 d.p.)

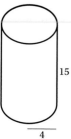

Start by working out the volume of water.

Volume of water bottle (cylinder)
= area of circular base × height

$753.98 \, \text{cm}^3 = 753.98 \, \text{ml}$

Volume of water in bottle (in ml).

$753.98 \, \text{ml} \div 100 \, \text{ml} \times 2 = 15$ scoops

10 **a** $1:8$

Ratio of teachers to students

$x:140$

Let number of teachers = x

$x = 140 \div 8 = 17.5$

Number of teachers must be a whole number

18 teachers

b $21 \times 8 = 168$

Every teacher can have 8 students to supervise

$168 - 140$

A total of 168 students can go

28 more students

Number of extra students

c $21:140$

Teachers : students

$3:20$

⑪ There are eight numbers: _ _ _ _ _ _ _ _

The biggest number is 16: _ _ _ _ _ _ _ 16

The mean is 7.5. This tells you that they all add up to
8 × 7.5 = 60

The range is 15. This means that the biggest minus the
smallest is 15, so the smallest is 1.

1 _ _ _ _ _ _ 16

The mode is 3 and 5. This tells you that there must
be more 3s and 5s than everything else and the same
number of 3s and 5s. There might be two of each or
three of each. If there are two of each you have:

1 3 3 5 5 _ _ 16

The total so far is 33, which means the other two
numbers must add up to 27 (because the mean tells
you that the eight numbers add up to 60). The other
two numbers can't be another 3 and a 5 (because they
only add up to 8).

The bigger of the two numbers must be 15 (because
if it was 16 then the mode would be 16 too) and the
other must be 12.

If the bigger one is 14 then the other one is 13.

1 3 3 5 5 12 15 16

1 3 3 5 5 13 14 16

What does each piece of information tell you?

Start putting the numbers in order.

12 **a**

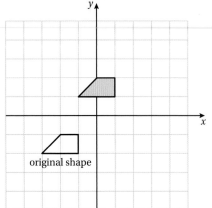

original shape

Tracing paper can help with notations.

b

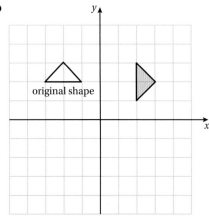

original shape

c

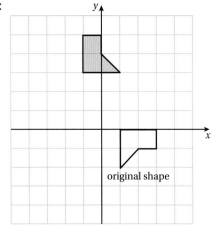

original shape

0.74	0.46	0.9
or	or	or
$\dfrac{74}{100}$	$\dfrac{46}{100} = \dfrac{23}{50}$	$\dfrac{90}{100} = \dfrac{9}{10}$
0.86	0.7	0.54
or	or	or
$\dfrac{129}{150} = \dfrac{43}{50} = \dfrac{86}{100}$	$\dfrac{70}{100} = \dfrac{7}{10}$	$\dfrac{54}{100} = \dfrac{27}{50}$
0.5	0.94	0.66
or	or	or
$\dfrac{50}{100} = \dfrac{1}{2}$	$\dfrac{94}{100} = \dfrac{47}{50}$	$\dfrac{33}{50} = \dfrac{66}{100}$

Remember that in a magic square all the rows and columns and both main diagonals add up to the magic number. The key idea here is to convert everything into the same type of number. It is easiest to work in either decimals or in fractions with a denominator of 100. The diagram shows possible answers: you only need one answer in each square.

a $100\,\text{cm} \times 80\,\text{cm} \times 70\,\text{cm} = 560\,000\,\text{cm}^3$

Volume of planter box. Work in cm because you need to know the volume in cm³.

$560\,000\,\text{cm}^3 = 560\,000\,\text{ml}$

Volume of planter box (in litres)

$560\,000\,\text{ml} = 560\,\text{litres}$

$560\,\text{litres} \div 50\,\text{litres} = 11.2$

So she will need 12 bags of compost to fill the planter box.

Number of bags of compost required. You can't round off like you would normally do because 11 bags won't be enough.

b $12 \div 3 = 4$

How many times can she use the special offer?

$4 \times £12 = £48$

Cost of 12 bags of compost, using the special offer.

c $12 \times £5.99 = £71.88$

Cost of 12 bags of compost at the regular price.

$£71.88 - £48 = £23.88$

Savings when she uses the special offer.

15

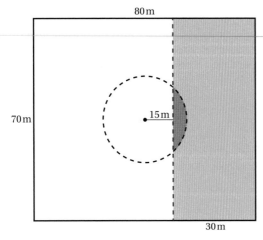

The shaded area shows the part the goat can eat.

You could draw a rectangle measuring 8 cm by 7 cm.

The goat is tethered on a rope measuring 15 m.

On this diagram, the locus of points within which the goat will be is a circle of radius 1.5 cm with the centre in the middle of the field.

Measure 3 cm from the end of the field to show where the wheat is planted.

16

a $\frac{4}{52} \times \frac{3}{51} = \frac{12}{2652} = \frac{1}{221}$

You could start by writing down the probability of picking one ace. Then, if you are lucky and have picked an ace, write down the probability of picking an ace when there are only 51 cards left.

b There are two red kings, so the probabilities are:

$\frac{2}{52} \times \frac{1}{51} = \frac{2}{2652}$

Picking two aces is 6 times as likely.

17

a $1 - (0.1 + 0.2 + 0.3 + 0.3)$

0.1

The probabilities should add up to 1.

b $0.1 \times 0.1 = 0.01$

c

A table might help.

+	4	5	6	7	8
4			10		
5		10			
6	10				
7					
8					16

$(0.3 \times 0.1) + (0.2 \times 0.2) + (0.1 \times 0.3)$

p(4 kits and 6 kits) = $0.1 \times 0.3 = 0.03$

p(5 kits and 5 kits) = $0.2 \times 0.2 = 0.04$

p(6 kits and 4 kits) = $0.3 \times 0.1 = 0.03$

Any of these outcomes are possible, so add them together to get 0.2

18 1 pint (imperial) is 0.568 litres (568 ml).

9 pints = 568 ml × 9 = 5112 ml

> We know there are two different units in the question: millilitres and pints.
>
> Here we have converted pints into millilitres.

5112 ml = approximately 5000 ml

= 5×10^3 ml of blood in James' body.

> The question asks you to work with approximate figures.

There are 5×10^9 red blood cells per millilitre of blood, so in total James has about $5 \times 10^9 \times 5 \times 10^3$

= $25 \times 10^{12} = 2.5 \times 10^{13}$ red blood cells

10% of $2.5 \times 10^{13} = 0.25 \times 10^{13}$

The number of remaining blood cells is
$2.5 \times 10^{13} - 0.25 \times 10^{13} = 2.25 \times 10^{13}$

19

> A clear, well-labelled diagram will be useful. This one focuses on the important triangle.

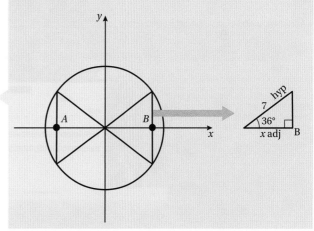

$OB = \cos 36° \times 7\,\text{cm} = 5.663...\,\text{cm}$

> To work out x you need to use trigonometry.

B: (5.66, 0)

> Now interpret this in terms of the coordinates of point B (values rounded up to 2 d.p. as required).

A: (−5.66, 0)

> Point A is a reflection of point B in the y axis.

GCSE
MATHEMATICS
online

The complete
online resource
for GCSE
Mathematics

GCSE Mathematics Online
for Edexcel is our brand
new interactive teaching
and learning subscription
service. This tablet-friendly
resource supports both
independent learning
and whole class teaching
through a suite of flexible
resources that includes
lessons, tasks, questions,
quizzes, widgets and games.

▷ Allows teachers to set tasks and tests, auto-mark and compile
reports to review student performance.

▷ A test generator so teachers can compile their own assessments.

▷ Interactive widgets to visually demonstrate concepts.

▷ Worksheets offering practical activities, discussion points,
investigations, games and further practice.

▷ Walkthroughs that take students through a question step-by-step,
with feedback.

▷ Quick-fire quizzes with leaderboards, providing an opportunity for
question practice.

▷ Levelled questions that assess understanding of each topic.

▷ Covers both Foundation and Higher, offering flexibility for moving
students between tiers.

▷ Resources organised into chapters corresponding to the Student
Books, with explanatory notes for all topics.

▷ Contains material for all types of classroom set-up, including
interactive whiteboards and projectors.

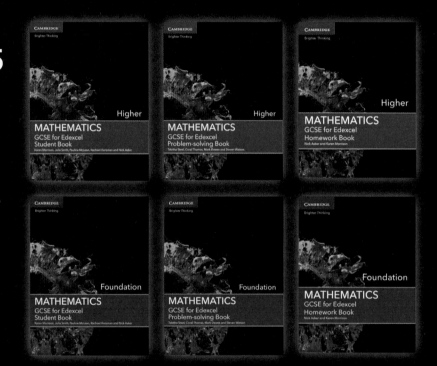